SIX SIGM

# About the ITSM Library

The publications in the ITSM Library cover best practice in IT Management and are published on behalf of itSMF Netherlands (itSMF-NL).

The IT Service Management Forum (itSMF) is the association for IT service organizations, and for customers of IT services. itSMF's goal is to promote innovation and support of IT management; suppliers and customers are equally represented within the itSMF. The Forum's main focus is exchange of peer knowledge and experience. Our authors are global experts.

The following publications are, or soon will be, available.

**Introduction, Foundations and Practitioners books**
- Foundations of IT Service Management based on ITIL® (Arabic, Chinese, German, English, French, Italian, Japanese, Korean, Dutch, Brazilian Portuguese, and Russian; Danish and Spanish to be delivered in Spring 2007)
- IT Services Procurement – an introduction based on ISPL (Dutch)
- Project Management based on PRINCE2™ 2005 Edition (Dutch, English, German)
- Release & Control for IT Service Management, based on ITIL® - A Practitioner Guide (English)

**IT Service Management – best practices**
- IT Service Management – best practices, part 1 (Dutch)
- IT Service Management – best practices, part 2 (Dutch)
- IT Service Management – best practices, part 3 (Dutch)
- IT Service Management – best practices, part 4 (Dutch)

**Topics & Management instruments**
- Metrics for IT Service Management (English)
- Six Sigma for IT Management (English)
- The RfP for IT Outsourcing – A Management Guide (Dutch)
- Service Agreements – A Management Guide (English)
- Frameworks for IT Management (English)
- IT Governance based on COBIT® – A Management Guide (English, German)

**Pocket guides**
- ISO/IEC 20000 – A Pocket Guide (English, German, Japanese, Italian, Spanish, formerly BS 15000 – A Pocket Guide)
- IT Services Procurement based on ISPL – A Pocket Guide (English)
- IT Service CMM – A Pocket Guide (English)
- IT Service Management – a summary based on ITIL® (Dutch)
- IT Service Management from Hell! (English)

For any further enquiries about ITSM Library, please visit www.itsmfbooks.com, http://en.itsmportal.net/en/books/itsm_library or www.vanharen.net.

# Six Sigma for
# IT Management

## A POCKET GUIDE

Van Haren
PUBLISHING

# Colophon

| | |
|---|---|
| Title: | Six Sigma for IT Management - A Pocket Guide |
| A publication of: | itSMF-NL |

This Pocket Guide is based on *Six Sigma for IT Management*
(Van Haren Publishing for itSMF-NL, 2006), which was written by:

| | |
|---|---|
| Lead author: | Sven den Boer |
| Co-authors: | Rajeev Andharia |
| | Melvin Harteveld |
| | Linh Chi Ho |
| | Patrick L. Musto |
| | Silvia Prickel |

For this Pocket Guide, Ms. Linh Chi Ho created the glossary with key Six Sigma
terminologies and concepts useful for IT Service Management. The text of the Pocket
Guide was reviewed by the authors team.

| | |
|---|---|
| Editors: | Jan van Bon (chief editor) |
| | Tieneke Verheijen (editor) |
| Publisher: | Van Haren Publishing, Zaltbommel, www.vanharen.net |
| ISBN(13): | 978 90 8753 029 7 |
| Edition: | First edition, first impression, March 2007 |
| Design & Layout: | CO2 Premedia, Amersfoort - NL |
| Printer: | Wilco, Amersfoort - NL |

ITIL® is a Registered Trade Mark and a Community Trademark of the Office of Government
Commerce
Note: This pocket guide is based on ITILv2 and prior. ITIL version 3 is expected in 2007.
For any further enquiries about Van Haren Publishing, please send an e-mail to: info@vanharen.net

# Acknowledgments

*Six Sigma for IT Management - A Pocket Guide* would not have been possible without the 'Six Sigma for IT Management' book that was created as a 'global best practice' by the united efforts of Six Sigma experts all around the world. The Management Summary provided by this pocket guide has been extensively reviewed by the original authoring team, and we adjusted the text as they suggested.

This authoring team was gathered by a worldwide Call for Authors and Reviewers and includes:
- Sven den Boer (Lead Author) - Getronics Corporate, the Netherlands
- Rajeev Andharia - Sun Microsystems, India
- Melvin Harteveld - Getronics Corporate, the Netherlands
- Linh Chi Ho - Proxima Technology, USA
- Patrick L. Musto - ITSM Process Architect, USA
- Silvia Prickel - United Airlines, USA.

Sven den Boer acted as Lead Author of the original book and also participated in the selection of the Co-Authors. Sven is a trained Six Sigma Black Belt, was extensively trained in ITIL, and has broad experience in improving (IT) processes with the help of Six Sigma within Getronics, thus saving millions of dollars. Sven is co-Founder and Managing Director of ProjectsOne, a prime Business Process Improvement company in the Netherlands. ProjectsOne specializes in turn key Lean Six Sigma implementations for a broad range of companies and organizations. Besides his broad experience in Six Sigma, Sven is also specialized as a (PRINCE2) Project Manager and Professional Coach.

His colleague and co-author Melvin Harteveld supports Six Sigma as co-Founder of ProjectsOne. As a certified Black Belt and trained Master Black Belt, he has an in-depth knowledge of the Six Sigma improvement theory and the use of statistics to measure and improve processes in general.

Linh C. Ho is the Marketing Director at Proxima Technology where she helped Proxima become the first Service Management software vendor to include Six Sigma capabilities. Linh has also written articles and spoken at conferences on integrating these two approaches. She holds a Honors Baccalaureate in Commerce; International Business Management and Management Information Systems from the University of Ottawa, Canada. Linh wishes to thank Owen Berkeley-Hill (Ford Motor Company), Tim Young (Netezza), Steve Jones (Proxima Technology), Bryce Dunn (Proxima Technology), Dr. Jean Couillard Ph. D. (University of Ottawa) and Jon Efford (Plan-Net) for their support. For this pocket guide, she wrote an additional glossary on the commonly used Six Sigma terminology for IT Management. We would also like to thank Linh for copy-editing the complete manuscript of the Pocket Guide.

Patrick Musto joined the team as an ITSM Process Architect, Consultant, Practitioner and Trainer; he has over 25 years of leadership experience as a principal in a marketing research firm, director of quality for a global shared services organization and vice president of quality of information technology for an international financial concern. Patrick holds an MS in information and communication sciences, is trained as a Six Sigma Black Belt, is a member of the American Society for Quality (ASQ) and is a certified Manager in IT Service Management (ITIL). He has demonstrated experience in Business Process Improvement and process design and management and has served as a process architect for a Service Oriented Architecture (SOA) project. We would like to thank Patrick for his thorough reviews on the manuscript of this pocket guide.

Silvia Prickel joined the team as a certified Manager in IT Service Management (ITIL), ISO 20000 consultant and Six Sigma Black Belt. She has more than 25 years of IT experience and was selected as the 'Best of the Best' Black Belt by the American Society for Quality (ASQ) in 2001. In her current role of Managing Director of Service Support for United Airlines at Corporate Headquarters in Elk Grove, Illinois, she has accountability for day-to-day operational support functions and responsibility for all ITIL processes. Leveraging her knowledge and experience as a Six Sigma Blackbelt, Silvia has successfully streamlined several ITIL processes such as Change Management, Incident Management and Problem Management.

From another side of the world came Rajeev Andharia, a Project Management Professional (PMP), Certified Information Systems Auditor (CISA), Certified Manager in IT Service Management (ITIL), and a Certified Information System Security Professional (CISSP), who had more than eleven years of experience in IT consulting, project management and execution. Rajeev is familiar with many frameworks, among them ITIL and Six Sigma. The force behind Rajeev's contribution was the unwavering support of his friend and wife Shital. An MBA herself, Shital is an IT professional specializing in training and consulting. In addition to providing valuable inputs and quality reviews, Shital supported the project by spending weekends with Rajeev to create the chapter on IT process improvement.

Tieneke Verheijen, the expert editor co-ordinating the work on the original title on behalf of itSMF-NL, created this pocket guide with the core knowledge of the original publication, and co-ordinated the subsequent review. Jan van Bon, as itSMF-NL's chief editor, supervised this process and made sure that the resulting summary meets itSMF's requirements.

The original publication was reviewed by a large Quality Assurance Team, that was composed of a wide variety of professionals from all over the world:
- Rolf Akker - Atos Origin, the Netherlands
- Tercio Annunciado - CNH Latin America LTDA, Brazil
- Tim Ganguly - JPM-Guardian Installation Protection Program (IPP), USA
- Andreas Gräf - Hewlett-Packard GmbH, Germany
- Kadri Hasbay - Gap Inc, USA

- Steve Jones - Proxima Technology, USA
- Nari Kannan - Ajira Technologies Inc., USA
- Ricardo Mansur - Empreendimentos Mansur, Brazil
- Alex Tito de Morais - Fujitsu, Brazil
- Sandeep Narang - Pepperweed Consulting, USA
- Peter Ober - Hewlett-Packard GmbH, Germany
- Ulrich Erik Redmann - Vattenfall Europe Information Services GmbH, Germany
- Mart Rovers - InterProm USA Corporation, USA
- Adam Schlesinger - Microsoft Corporation, USA
- Steve Tremblay - Excelsa Technologies Consulting Inc., Canada
- Peter Westerhof - Compulegal.nl, the Netherlands
- Tim Young - Netezza, USA

We would like to thank them for all their efforts once again.

Given the desire for a broad consensus in the IT Service Management field, new developments, additional material and other contributions from IT Service Management professionals are welcome, to extend and further improve this publication. Any forwarded material will be discussed by the editorial team and, where appropriate, incorporated into new editions. Any comments can be sent to the chief editor, email: jan.van.bon@itsmf.nl.

Jan van Bon, Chief Editor on behalf of itSMF-NL
Tieneke Verheijen, Editor on behalf of itSMF-NL

# Foreword

There is overwhelming evidence that quality improvement processes really do increase customer satisfaction and operational efficiency (which results in measurable value to the business bottom line). Because of this, IT organizations have now added Six Sigma to ITIL processes. Since IT undoubtedly enables the business, improvement to IT services results in a direct and quantifiable improvement to the business processes they support.

Given that IT processes largely exist in an electronic universe where data capture and manipulation can be applied transparently with little or no human intervention, Six Sigma's statistical techniques and the plethora of IT data go hand in hand to help IT make more informed business decisions. It is often said that there's too much data and not enough information; Six Sigma helps transforming this data into business critical information - eg cost of poor quality, risk metrics.

Today, applications are self-incrementing and a wealth of tools exist to capture, consolidate and manipulate this data; it is a straightforward task to introduce a quality management layer to any IT service. Moreover, IT service management applications now contain Six Sigma techniques inherent in their solutions - making it even easier and more cost effective to benefit from Six Sigma techniques.

Six Sigma is gaining popularity in nearly every industry today, and has clear measurable successes widely recognized beyond the manufacturing organizations where it has its roots. Organizations such as Bank of America, American Express, Sun Microsystems and Getronics among others have realized tangible value from Six Sigma in IT.

This pocket guide is based on the '*Six Sigma for IT Management*' book; it is intended to help IT professionals understand the basics of Six Sigma for IT Service Management. Six Sigma techniques and concepts key to IT Management are covered in the following chapters. It is a great pleasure to be one of the co-authors of the original *'Six Sigma for IT Management'* book and to work with a team of Six Sigma and ITIL experts from around the world.


Linh C. Ho
Co-Author
Six Sigma for IT Management

# Contents

# Introduction

Delivering high quality IT services at minimum cost to the business continues to be a priority for IT executives. Because IT has become such an integral part of the business and its critical business processes, the need to align the business objectives with IT is crucial. The question is: how? How can IT be the enabler to improve the business and its processes? How can IT prove its added value to the business?

This is where quality improvement methodologies such as Six Sigma and best practices like ITIL can further help to bridge the gap between IT and the business. Moreover, combining these approaches helps IT to focus on strategic activities supporting business goals instead of dealing with day-to-day operations reactively.

This pocket guide gives an appreciation and insight into:
- what Six Sigma is
- how it can be used together with ITIL best practices, Total Quality Management and the IT process improvement approach
- when to utilize and combine these methods
- why IT managers should consider these approaches
- who should use Six Sigma
- practical techniques enabling IT professionals to immediately apply them in their IT organization
- common challenges to be aware of, and mistakes to avoid when implementing Six Sigma

Though Six Sigma is not IT focused, it does provide a consistent framework for measuring process outcomes for products and services. It is particularly useful in complementing the IT Infrastructure Library (ITIL) process approach, the de facto standard for managing IT organizations today. Though ITIL provides a set of best practices to deliver and support IT services, it does not quantify the quality of service performance or

how to improve it. It does urge IT Service Organizations to have a Service
Improvement Program (SIP), but it does not explain how they should
operate such a program in practice. Questions such as 'How do I collect
data?', 'What data should I collect?' and 'How can I draw any conlusions
from them?' are not answered. The *Planning to Implement Service Management* book and other published ITSM books and reports name Six Sigma
as a complementary quality improvement approach to ITIL processes.[1]

> *ITIL defines the 'what' of Service Management and Six Sigma defines the
> 'how' of process improvement.*

Together ITIL and Six Sigma are a perfect fit for improving the quality of
IT service delivery and support. The Six Sigma approach is well positioned
to provide quantifiable measures of process performance outcomes and
a consistent approach through the DMAIC (Define, Measure, Analyze,
Improve and Control) quality improvement cycle, in how and when to use
the metrics.

This pocket guide summarizes the 'Six Sigma for IT Management' book,
which was the first book to provide a coherent view and guidance for using
Six Sigma in IT service organizations. The book content has been adjusted
to fit the pocket guide format, chapters of the book have been summarized
and merged, while the case studies have been left out. Valuable techniques
from the case studies are summarized in the Appendix C.

Chapter 1 highlights the natural use of Six Sigma in IT Service
Management organizations, and is followed by Chapter 2 explaining Six
Sigma in detail. Chapter 3 summarizes ITIL and how it can be aligned
with Six Sigma. Chapter 4 merges the Six Sigma approach with the IT
process improvement view. Appendix A provides a glossary containing

---

1  *Planning to Implement Service Management* by Office of Government Commerce (OGC)
   (London 2002).

terminologies that are used in this book, while Appendix B contains an overview of the DMAIC phases including respective tasks. Appendix C suggests project techniques, with Appendix D completing the book with suggested further reading.

# What is Six Sigma?

The method owes its name to the Greek character sigma, 'σ'. In statistics, this letter represents the standard deviation, which indicates the amount of variation or inconsistency in a process. In the mid-eighties, Motorola introduced the statistical measurement of its process outcome, the measure of six times sigma, which means that in every million opportunities there are 3.4 defects.

> *The sigma measure, σ, represents the standard deviation. Six Sigma means six times sigma, indicating 3.4 defects per million opportunities (DPMO).*

The Six Sigma method does not insist that every organization should strive for six sigma or 3.4 DPMO. It does provide a quantitative methodology of continual (process) improvement and reducing costs, by reducing the amount of variation in process outcomes to a level suitable for the given organization. It also pursues data-driven, fact-based decision-making in which decisions are tied to corporate objectives. And finally, it uses an implementation of measurement-based strategy that focuses on process improvement and variation reduction.

While using a statistical approach, Six Sigma accounts for the quality assurance part of quality management. The continual improvement part of quality management is covered by the **DMAIC** quality improvement cycle:

- Define
- Measure
- Analyze
- Improve
- Control

Each of the DMAIC phases has clear objectives, tasks and techniques, that are explained in Chapter 2. At some companies an additional *Reporting* step is added to the model; though this is not a formal part of the Six Sigma DMAIC model, it is clear that reporting should take place in a structured way. This will also create exposure and enable you to share your success.

With the quality assurance covered by the statistical measurement approach and the continual improvement covered by the DMAIC cycle, you might conclude that Six Sigma is a Total Quality Management approach. This is explained further in Chapter 1: Why Six Sigma for IT Service Management?

## Why Six Sigma?

Six Sigma enables organizations to streamline their processes by reducing the number of defects or the amount of waste, and to raise their customer satisfaction. Figure 0.1 shows a process outline and the waste in a process: jobs that are not done right the first time take extra time to put right. The rework can be seen as waste and is also called 'the hidden organization'. By making this visible, Six Sigma helps management to make decisions: what parts of a process should be improved and how?

By first detecting, tackling and solving the issues that affect the business most, the value of an organization is increased exactly where it can be increased the most. On average, companies spend 20% of their revenue on the hidden organization, but a company at Six Sigma level in its processes spends significantly less.

Thus, Six Sigma will allow you to prove success in a project from its start, through the use of consequent measurement. This represents a huge potential shown by virtually no other technology, providing a very good starting point for your projects.

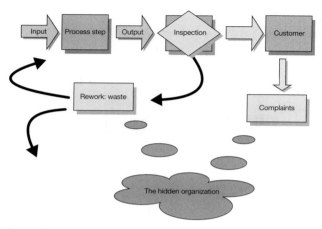

Figure 0.1 Waste in an organizational process

Finally, Six Sigma will also help you to grow your organization's skill-set as it will reveal weaknesses and provide tools to close the gaps.

## Who should use Six Sigma?

Each organization wishing to optimize its IT-dependant business processes can and should use Six Sigma. Various types of organizations have already proven its benefits and possibilities of adaptation. The financial industry, for example, focused on the core business processes, as these are nearly the same for all market players of this segment. Pharmaceutical companies, driven by the regulations of the US Food and Drug Administration (FDA), implemented Six Sigma to control their activities in this area. The government sector started Six Sigma activities a little later, but these go throughout their whole organization.

The techniques of Six Sigma can also be applied to identify and improve critical (IT) process areas in your IT organization. Six Sigma forces you to turn a process or organizational problem into a statistical problem that can be measured (Figure 0.2). These measurements give management information to base their decision on an operational solution for the problem. Using this approach organizations are spending less than 5% of revenue on what we call the hidden organization, when they have reached Six Sigma level (Figure 0.1).

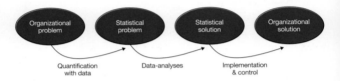

Figure 0.2 Fact-based decision-making

## How to use Six Sigma

Deployed correctly, Six Sigma does not end; it becomes a way of life, thus ensuring the best results for any organization. The continual improvement ideas of Juran and Deming reflecting this idea will be introduced in Chapter 1.

In a number of cases, Six Sigma has become a tactical project focus on improvements using DMAIC methodology. In this situation, Six Sigma is viewed as a short-term 'quick win' and acceptance of the philosophy is never realized. As a result, the true value of Six Sigma as a holistic improvement effort fails to be realized.

## Aligning Six Sigma with ITIL

ITIL was developed in the 1980s, by the British Government's Central Computer and Telecommunications Agency (CCTA).[2] It was based on the premise that spending on IT in government was becoming too high, and a method to establish best practice processes for IT Service Management would be of benefit. ITIL became the de facto standard for IT Service

---

2  Now known as the Office of Government Commerce (OGC).

Management. The book and this pocket guide are based on ITILv2. The framework can be used to assist organizations in developing their IT Service Management (ITSM) process-driven approaches. ITIL recognizes five principal elements in providing IT services, of which Service Delivery and Service Support are the most widely adopted elements. They are explained further in Chapter 3.

Though Six Sigma and ITIL are often used independently, this pocket guide suggests a way to gain the best of both worlds, using the process approach from ITIL and the improvement model from Six Sigma. In order to combine ITIL and Six Sigma, the two need to be aligned. This should be approached as a project, in the same way as you align IT with business objectives. Chapter 3 and 4 explain how this can be done. Of course you should always take your organization's culture into account, together with the process and investment aspects.

In this respect we distinguish four types of organizations:
• organizations using both ITIL and Six Sigma
• organizations using ITIL without using Six Sigma techniques
• organizations using Six Sigma but not using ITIL
• organizations using neither approach

This book is particularly aimed at companies in the last three scenarios; therefore we elaborate on these in Chapter 3. In this chapter, we also expand on how ITIL best practices can be placed within the DMAIC model.

Common Six Sigma techniques used in ITIL environments are Service Improvement Program (SIP), Voice of the Customer (VOC), Pareto charts, Failure Mode and Effects Analysis, control charts and process sigma value. SIP is already embedded in both Six Sigma and ITIL. Appendix C contains a list recommending more valuable techniques.

## Summary

While Six Sigma is not an IT focused framework, it does provide a consistent framework for measuring and improving the quality of services and products. Six Sigma is complementary to the IT Infrastructure Library (ITIL) best practices by quantifying and continually improving the quality of IT services delivered to the business.

> *ITIL defines the 'what' of Service Management and Six Sigma defines the 'how' of process improvement.*

> *The sigma measure, σ, represents the standard deviation. Six Sigma means six times sigma, indicating 3.4 defects per million opportunities (DPMO).*

This is not an arbitrary measure for which every organization should strive. The most important aspect of the methodology is the quantitative and **DMAIC** structured approach for continual (process) improvement and reducing costs, thereby enabling data-driven, fact-based decision-making tied to corporate objectives.

Each organization wishing to optimize its IT-dependant business processes should adopt Six Sigma as part of the company culture. Combining ITIL and Six Sigma helps IT further align itself to the business and exceed its performance requirements.

# 1 Why Six Sigma for IT Service Management?

## 1.1 The importance of quality management

Business, as well as IT success, depends on how well they can deliver against mounting expectations of an increasingly demanding client base. It entails understanding their perspective on quality and value, and ensuring that the service is designed and managed to meet that perspective. This is what *quality management* is about.

Total Quality Management (TQM) aims at realizing quality. It is a generic term used to describe a vast collection of philosophies, concepts, methods, and tools - among them, Six Sigma. We will first explain TQM in general and the Six Sigma methodology in particular, and then see how Six Sigma, coupled with IT Service Management, is a powerful breakthrough for business and IT process management.

### 1.1.1 Total Quality Management (TQM)

> *"Quality is the totality of characteristics of a product or service that bear on its ability to satisfy stated and implied needs."* (ISO-8402)

From the beginning of the twentieth century, with the industrial revolution as its main driver, companies have been trying to control the quality of the products they were producing. After World War II, W. Edwards Deming and Joseph Juran both contributed tremendously to the development of TQM techniques.

Juran established three fundamental concepts of Total Quality Management:

- **Customer focus** - Customer satisfaction surveys of 4.3 out of 5 mean nothing. What truly matters is whether satisfaction rating is creating business or losing business. A continuous dialogue with the customer is essential to refine the services and to ensure that both the customer and the supplier know what is expected of the service. Section 1.2 discusses Six Sigma's Critical to Quality (CTQ) factors that can help establish this dialogue.

- **Continual improvement** - 'Continual improvement' is an important part of TQM. Deming's Quality Circle proved to be a simple and effective model to control and improve quality. It revolves around four principles of: *Plan, Do, Check, Act* (PDCA), see Figure 1.1. Using PDCA in a continuous cycle of improvements over time allows an organization to continuously mature its ability to drive quality in the services delivered:
  - *Plan* – what should be done, when should it be done, who should be doing it, how should it be done, and by using what
  - *Do* – the planned activities are implemented
  - *Check* – determine if the activities provided the expected result
  - *Act* – adjust the plans based on information gathered while checking
- **Value of every associate** - Employees influence change. When empowered, they become the greatest asset for improving quality. Empowering people improves employee satisfaction. Employee satisfaction improves productivity. A productive workplace stimulates innovation. Innovation fosters success! Total Quality Management must consider the 'people' aspect of the equation and often this emanates within the culture (the values and beliefs) of the organization. Influencing this requires a clear and consistent policy communicating to each employee how and to what extent their tasks contribute to realizing the organization's objectives. Then they can be empowered and accountable for carrying out those responsibilities.

## 1.2 Six Sigma for TQM

In order to get to the bottom line of every organizational problem, organizations need to measure value, as measurements carry relevance to every customer, every activity and every employee of an organization.

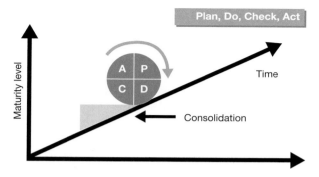

Figure 1.1 Deming's Quality Circle

But how do you measure quality and value? TQM measures quality as discrete functions. Six Sigma uses metrics to calculate the success of everything that an organization does.

> *Six Sigma focuses on Critical to Quality (CTQ) metrics following from customer requirements. Its end-to-end perspective allows for a total quality picture focused on the product, as well as the processes within the operation that produces the product.*

As a result, Six Sigma produces quality with far more tangible and financial results than the TQM approaches:

- up to 20 percent margin improvement
- a 12-18 percent increase in capacity
- a 12 percent reduction in the number of employees
- a 10-30 percent capital reduction

Six Sigma splits the production of a product or a service into a series of processes. All processes consist of a series of steps, events, or activities that achieve an objective or goal. Six Sigma measures every step of the process by breaking apart the elements within each process, identifying the critical characteristics, defining and mapping the related processes, understanding the capability of each process, discovering the weak links, and then upgrading the capability of the process. Only by taking these steps can a business raise the 'high-water mark' of its performance.

After this, the *Critical to Quality characteristics* (CTQs) become apparent. They define the output of the individual processes. Once defined and quantified, the variables (inputs) that affect the CTQs can be adjusted accordingly.

The key at this point is in determining which variables have the greatest impact on the outcome. This is statistically accomplished through 'Design of Experiments' and 'Probability'. Once the key variables (X) are identified and defined, measures can be taken to optimize and control. Thus, quality is improved *where it matters most* and *not for quality's sake*.

Six Sigma furthermore unveils variations within the process. Once identified, these variables can then be controlled so that they are predictable, repeatable and consistent. This ensures continuous customer satisfaction and significantly reduces operating costs.

The methodology for managing this is through Six Sigma's DMAIC cycle (Define, Measure, Analyze, Improve, Control).

It is important to note that Critical to Quality (CTQ) translates to 'Critical to Satisfaction' from the customer's perspective. Improving CTQs therefore requires linking to customer needs (Figure 1.2).

> *In summary, Six Sigma is the measurement of processes used to deliver a service or a product where critical-to-quality factors are optimized and brought under control in order to meet or exceed customer satisfaction.*

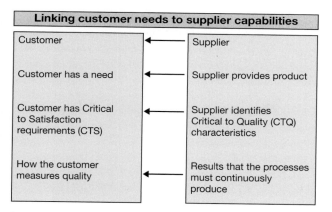

**Linking customer needs to supplier capabilities**

| Customer | Supplier |
|----------|----------|
| Customer has a need | ← Supplier provides product |
| Customer has Critical to Satisfaction requirements (CTS) | ← Supplier identifies Critical to Quality (CTQ) characteristics |
| How the customer measures quality | ← Results that the processes must continuously produce |

Figure 1.2 Linking customer needs to supplier capabilities

## 1.3 What is Service Management?

While Six Sigma is used to measure 'how' the inputs and outputs of a process can be optimized, we must also consider 'what' processes are necessary to deliver the service.

> **Service Management** is an alignment of strategy with objectives, processes, and procedures that drives delivery of services to the customer.

This alignment of strategy is critical in understanding 'what' processes are required for the delivery of a service.

The key components in Service Management are:
- **Alignment** - The business and IT should agree upon what business and strategy indicators there are for IT to align with (for example, if the business wants to outsource parts of the production, then this is an indication for IT to prepare for integrating suppliers in business processes and systems). In Six Sigma terms, this is referenced from the customer's perspective as 'Critical to Satisfaction'.

- **Replication** - The most powerful way to accelerate dramatically the results of quality and productivity improvement efforts is the ability to replicate quickly across the organization. Resistance to change, the 'not invented here' syndrome, or the 'every location is different' excuse are three of the main challenges to be overcome here. Successful companies make replication an obligation, not an option. Creating an environment that is scalable and agile, where processes and procedures can be quickly and easily replicated, will foster success in the business.

- **Linkage (process management)** - A common theme carried throughout this chapter is to link processes from an 'end-to-end' perspective, and to measure performance in terms of inputs and outputs. Service Management also focuses on linking processes. The single most important factor that must be considered in every process is the customer. A company may be a collection of processes, but the customer only sees it in terms of the output of those processes. All he wants is a product that meets his needs and requirements at the agreed time for the agreed price. In order to meet these requirements, the organization must link all activities transparently, in such a way that the output meets the expectations. Process mapping is a powerful tool used in Six Sigma to gain an understanding of the activities necessary to produce an outcome. The final outcome must always be from a customer's perspective. Process mapping can be used to identify key value-add activities from those activities that provide little to no value and can be eliminated to produce a more efficient process (see section 4.6).

When you combine strategy, replication and process management you have Service Management. When you combine Service Management with the power of Six Sigma, you have a well defined, controlled set of efficient processes to deliver a product or service that consistently meets and exceeds customer satisfaction.

# 1.4   IT Service Management and Six Sigma

> *IT Service Management is: the whole of principles and practices of designing, delivering and maintaining IT services to an agreed level of quality, in support of a Customer activity.*

The *objectives* of *IT Service Management* are *alignment* by *customer focus* and *delivering quality*. *Six Sigma* focuses on *customer* and *quality* as well, *through the use of metrics*. It will provide value to IT Service Management in the following ways (see Figure 1.3):

- **Gauge process performance through measurements and applied statistics** - the process (for example, break-fix service under a Service Level Agreement) can be monitored in a very sophisticated way, namely by a control chart (see Appendix A and C).
- **Improve process efficiency in a concrete and effective way** - the Six Sigma method to improve your business processes is unique: it relies on solid data and measurement. There is room for intuition at the start of an improvement project, and although Six Sigma involves some mathematical calculations, the vast amount of tools available in the market to automate these calculations helps Six Sigma beginners to learn it. The broad spectrum of analytical tools and techniques allows for problem-solving capabilities that are simply unsurpassed. They leave no room for confusion or ambiguity and can be transformed into crystal-clear benefits in terms of financials and customer satisfaction.
- **Defining and quantifying customer needs** - CTQs provide us with an understanding of what the customer expects our process to deliver. By aligning our process objectives and the CTQs through customer needs mapping, we not only understand what the customer considers important, but are positioned to measure how the process is performing relative to what the customer expects. By leveraging Process Capability Analysis (PCA) we can assess the capability of our process. Process capability, as measured by a PCA, provides a means to understand how a

process normally behaves considering the variables that normally impact the process. By analyzing the process capability, we can determine if the process will deliver to the CTQs or if an improvement of the process will be necessary.

- **Predict process behavior instead of reacting to it** - Six Sigma identifies the root causes for process behavior and thus allows for proactive controlling of these factors, enabling a much better control over the process. A mathematical equation can be issued which will predict *at least 80%* of process behavior. This allows the process to be steered upfront, instead of correcting any mistakes later, and avoids mistakes and dissatisfied customers, saving time, money and reputations.

- **Helps to distinguish between every day fluctuations and signals that need your attention** - Six Sigma gives us the root causes for process behavior in a mathematical equation and it allows us to calculate the lower and upper limits that these root causes may take when affecting the process in order to stay within customer or company specifications on process output. Controlling these inputs on a control chart allows for very rapid signalling when action is required.

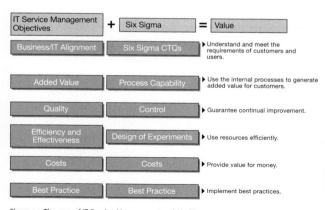

Figure 1.3 The sum of IT Service Management and Six Sigma

# 1.5  Summary

> *If you don't measure it, you can't control it.*
> *If you don't control it, you can't improve it.*
> *If you don't improve it, your company will not survive.*

TQM is not simply a means of conforming to specifications and requirements, it is a means of meeting and even exceeding needs and expectations of customers through customer focus, continual improvement and employee empowerment. Management of processes through organizational alignment and replication evolves TQM into Service Management.

Six Sigma is a very specific form of Total Quality Management, getting to the bottom line of organizational problems by metrical fact-finding and improving quality where it matters most. Its integrated, holistic and coherent approach provides the means to measure 'how' IT Service Management processes deliver against the customer expectations of their services. Six Sigma does not merely measure the outcome, but also measures the factors that go into Service Management performance: the drivers of performance. This approach empowers the process owner to control and continually improve the process. Combining Service Management and Six Sigma provides a powerful breakthrough for business and IT process management!

# 2 What is Six Sigma?

Motorola is generally considered to be the company to have taken the first steps with Dr Maikel Harry and engineer Bill Smith in driving Six Sigma forward. In the mid-eighties, Chairman Bob Glavin embraced the value and subsequent cultural and educational embedding of Six Sigma in the company. This allowed Six Sigma to develop into a mature methodology with a solid scientific basis. It has, thus, become a way of doing business instead of using a toolbox.

Although Six Sigma has its roots in manufacturing, today the banking world and various services companies acknowledge the value of the supporting techniques. The method spread throughout Europe and worldwide at a slow, but very steady, pace.

The initiative was born out of a quality practice that did not provide sufficient precision to assess the performance of some high technology processes and products. The company therefore introduced the famous defect per *million opportunities* measurement, which allowed them to put more detail and refinement into quality analysis, resulting in attacking the root causes of failures instead of traditionally combating the symptoms.

In fact, this only further extended on work done by earlier quality management 'gurus'. The Six Sigma measurement of 3.4 defects per million opportunities can be mathematically traced back to the invention of normal distribution in the early 19th century by Carl Frederick Gauss (1777-1855).

*If a certain amount of information (data points) about, for example, product performance is distributed in such a way that the most frequently occurring value is in the middle of the range and other probabilities tail off symmetrically in both directions, we speak of a normal distribution.*

This sort of distribution is graphically shown by a bell-shaped curve, like Figure 2.3. Due to its inventor's name, it is also called a Gauss curve. In a range of normally distributed data, the mean and median are very close and may be identical.

The next big step was set by Walter Shewhart in the 1920s when he showed that processes need adjustments when they step out of the three sigma bandwidth, thus creating a basis for Six Sigma terms like Process Capability Index (Cpk), signal, and control charts.[1]

Various process optimization techniques were matched by numerical production control techniques. Where process optimization focused on the elimination of waste, production was also focused on numerical control.

The other statistical tooling within Six Sigma originates from classical (example: Two-sample T-test) and modern (General Linear Model, ICC-Kappa-test) mathematics and statistics. This does not qualify the method as unique. What truly sets it apart is its ability to bring all this tooling under one banner in twelve clear steps to success, making these techniques available to every employee.

## 2.1 Definition of Six Sigma

There are two meanings to the actual term Six Sigma:
• a yardstick for quality and a symbol to aim for
• a mathematically derived number to assess the first pass yield of a process

The yardstick refers to the fact that many companies strive to avoid errors in their own processes of manufacturing or service providing. This instils a sense of perfection in the staff involved, and it avoids consuming time and money in rework and additional inspection cost, let alone in waste products.

---

1 Walter Shewhart, Economic Control of Quality of Manufactured Product (New York 1931).

The yardstick is thus an element of company culture rather than a numerical tool.

The second meaning fills in the numbers quite elegantly, stating for each process or chain of processes (value stream) exactly what that long term and short term sigma number will be. We shall take a closer look at what really happens here:

1. **Process definition** - the process to be measured has to be defined in terms of *scope and specification limits.*
2. **Measurements** - a sufficient number of representative and valid measurements must be taken.
3. This will allow us to determine the **mean**, the **standard deviation** as well as the form of **distribution**, for example, a normal distribution:
   - *mean* is an estimate of the average value in a population.
   - *standard deviation* is an estimate of the spread around an average in a population.
   - *distribution* is a curve which states the chances of an outcome occurring in the population based on the mean and the standard deviation. As it is a distribution of chance, the sum under the entire curve must equal 100%. The shape of the curve can take different forms. As these forms differ, multiple distributions are available to us, of which the normal distribution is best known. Time related data usually takes the form of a Weibull distribution. The type of distribution will often dictate the type of statistical tests and analysis to be utilized.
   - *upper and lower specification limit (USL/LSL)* is an outcome of a process which is acceptable to the customer. For example, 90% of computer malfunctions will be solved within a four-hour timeframe.
   - *first pass yield* is the number of outcomes that have been run through the process for the first time without any failures per 100.
4. **Determine the sigma value of the process** - given the mean, its standard deviation and the distribution form, we can compute the

percentage of products, services, or process runs that will fall within our specification limits. This can then be converted to a sigma value.

> *The sigma measure, σ, represents the standard deviation. Six Sigma means six times sigma, indicating 3.4 defects per million opportunities (DPMO).*

The example below shows how this can be done.

## 2.2 Example: Time to fix a customer call about a defective laptop

> In a given organization, the IT department and the business have agreed to set the times to fix laptops in their SLAs. Now the IT department wants to measure whether the target times are met, in order to report to the business about its performance.

1. **Process definition:** under the contract, customers will be helped in less than one hour with all laptop problems they experience.
2. **Measurements:** 30 laptop problems will be independently timed from the moment a customer reports the problem to the moment a customer agrees on the fixing of that problem.
3. **The measurements yield the following information:**
   - *mean*: 54.14 minutes
   - *standard deviation*: 3.5 minutes
   - *distribution form*: the distribution has been tested and yields the normal form
   - *Upper specification limit (USL)*: 60 minutes
   - *Lower specification limit (LSL)*: 0 minutes (boundary)

As all the dotted values fall within the boundary lines, which form the bandwith for the normal distribution, it is safe to conclude that the data is normally distributed.

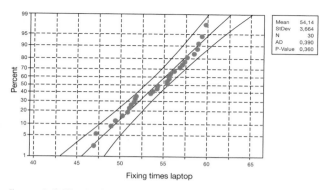

Figure 2.1 Probability plot of fixing times for laptops (Normal - 95 % Confidence Interval)

Figure 2.2 shows a 'heartbeat' of the process, where each of the thirty data points is stated in time order. The middle line states the average of 54.14 minutes. The lines above and below this line state the limits of control. If any data point is outside these control limits, the chances are more than 99% that there is a special cause which needs investigation and/or remedy.

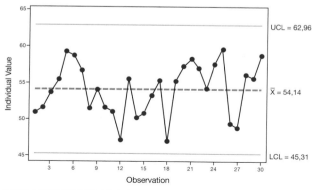

Figure 2.2 Chart of fixing times for laptops

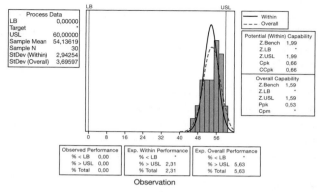

Figure 2.3 Process capability of fixing times for laptops

## 2.2.1 Calculate sigma value

Now, the corresponding sigma value can be calculated and yields 1.99 sigma in the short term and 1.59 sigma in the long term. The curve of the process has been estimated, as well as average and standard deviation. Predictions can be made on the short term and long term performance of the process.

What does this tell us? First, that out of 1,000,000 calls, 23,100 calls will not be fixed within the hour as the process performs today. Or, put differently, that 2.31% of all calls will not be solved within the one-hour deadline. This corresponds to 1.99 sigma.

Secondly, we learn that in the long run performance may get worse due to the fact that processes tend to drift at plus or minus 1.5 sigma in time. Here, we have to assume a worst case scenario, and therefore the predicted long term percentage of calls missed increases to 5.63%, corresponding to 1.59 sigma. So, in this example, the process does not even come near to performing on a Six Sigma level.

But does it have to? The answer is usually *no, it does not*. It depends entirely on the agreement with the customer. If a 90% service level agreement has been signed, an actual long term service of 94.37% satisfies the contractual terms fully.

To sum up, Six Sigma is a term to express our striving for operational excellence and control; it provides us with a numerical tool objectively to assess and compare the performance of processes in both the long and the short term. It is by no means necessary to attain a Six Sigma performance for all processes, as this is fully dependent on the situation.

## 2.3  Reduce variation

It is important to consider that customers do not care about average service levels. When they have excellent service one day and very bad service the next, they cannot *rely* on the process' performance because it's inconsistent.

It is the spread (unpredictability and inconsistency) that dissatisfies customers, not the average of the process. Moreover, a process with an average within customer specifications may still yield a lot of waste due to too large a variation. In general, customers hate surprises, as do managers and employees.

The true qualities of a product, service or process depend on the location of the *mean* (average) and its *variation* (spread) in relation to the lower specification limit (LSL) and the upper specification limit (USL).

A scenario where the spread is too large or the location of the mean is not well centered between LSL and USL will cause defects, complaints, inspection costs, rework, etc. This is called the 'hidden factory' or the 'hidden services organization'.

> *The bigger the process variation (spread), the bigger the costs.*

In general, we need to work out customer needs and translate these into upper and lower specification limits (USL and LSL). The process must then be altered to stay within those specification limits at all times. This increases the predictability of the process and the customer will feel that the process is dependable. It increases customer satisfaction and reduces inspection, rework and waste costs.

## 2.4 DMAIC walk-through

Instead of using the above techniques at random, Six Sigma uses a consistent approach to improving quality — called the DMAIC:

1. Define
2. Measure
3. Analyze
4. Improve
5. Control

'Report' is not a formal step in the DMAIC, however, Reporting about project results and documenting processes should take place in a structured way. There is some thoughts described in this chapter about the *Report* step within the Control phase.

There is a system behind these steps, which mimics the methodology applied when conducting scientific research. In essence, this consists of defining the research, ensuring that the object of research can be measured, conducting measurements and proving or rejecting hypothesis on the test subject before writing up the findings.

### 2.4.1 DMAIC: **Define (1)**

In this step, the subject of the project is defined in a very specific way. The following terms define a Six Sigma project:

- **External CTQ (Critical to Quality)** - this term describes the broad outline of the goal of the project – for example, 'we need to decrease sick leave'. It reflects what the customer wants to get out of the project. The importance of assessing the needs of the customer and reflecting these in the external Critical to Quality parameter (CTQ) cannot be over-emphasized.

- **Internal CTQ** - the internal CTQ (Int CTQ) describes in quantifiable terms how the external CTQ could be measured. For example, sick leave = (number of days on sick leave in a week/number of workable days in the same week)*100%. Now the external CTQ can be quantified by using the definition of the internal CTQ. The project goal takes a better shape, for example 'reduce sick leave to 3% for the year 2006'. It is of vital importance that the internal CTQ relates directly to the external CTQ, with the two having a one to one relationship.

- **Unit** - the unit denotes the object of which the internal CTQ is an attribute. If we were to report the sick leave percentage on a weekly basis, the unit of measurement would be the sick leave percentage of a single week for the entire population. An attribute of a week of workable days is its percentage of days on sick leave.

- **Defects and opportunities** - a defect needs an opportunity to occur. In our example, an opportunity is a workable day for one employee. This employee could report sick (defect) or not. The workable day itself is the opportunity as it has two outcomes: defect (sick) or no defect (not sick). The number of defects per million opportunities denotes the quality of any given process.

- **Population** - all opportunities included in the scope of the project constitute the population. For example, 'all workable days for the year 2006 from departments A, B, and D'. This population can be divided into 52 units each with a weekly percentage of sick leave.

When all the above terms have been defined and agreed upon, the project can be continued to the *Measure* phase.

## 2.4.2  ᴰᴹᴬᴵᶜ: **Measure (2)**

Obtaining a good and reliable set of data is the goal here. The definitions of the internal CTQ (Int CTQ) and unit are transformed into a process of measurements. The single most important consideration is whether the measurement procedure will provide accurate and dependable data to be analyzed. In order to establish this, a number of issues must be checked:

- **Validity** - is the measurement reflecting the object and/or attribute that you want to measure?
- **Bias** - are there any factors influencing the measurements, causing the population or process being measured to appear different from what it actually is? Bias is introduced into a measure when data is collected without regard to key factors that may influence it.
- **Stability** - is the measurement susceptible to trends and fluctuations in time (long term)?
- **Resolution** - can the object be measured with a sufficient degree of detail and accuracy? The resolution of your design defines the amount of information that can be provided by the design of experiment.
- **Linearity** - are there significant deviations in measurements at extremes of the outcome spectrum? Linearity is the variation between a known standard, or 'truth', across the low and high end of the range of measurements. The difference between an individual's measurements and that of a known standard or truth over the full range of expected values indicates the linearity of these measurements.
- **Repeatability** - if the measurement is repeated under exactly the same conditions, is the result still the same? Repeatability is the variation in measurements obtained when one person takes multiple measurements using the same instrument and techniques on the same parts or items.
- **Reproducibility** - if the measurement is repeated under different conditions, are the results within acceptable deviations? Reproducibility is the variation in average measurements obtained when several persons measure the same parts or items using the same technique of measuring.

All these issues require careful consideration. If even one of them does not fall within the limits of tolerance of measurement error, the procedure, method, and/or tooling must be adjusted. Overlooking potential problems

at this stage is one of the most common mistakes and will prove fatal for
the project every time.

Without a solid set of data, further analysis is pointless and the project
comes to a full stop.

## 2.4.3 DMAIC: **Analyze (3)**

Now a good quality set of data is available and the current capability of the
unaltered process can be assessed. In addition, the final project goals can
be determined. For example: a given problem should occur 80% less often
than before. Then potential influence factors can be listed.

Before a process capability analysis can be performed a number of issues
need to be checked:

- **Control chart** - this is the heartbeat of your process and will depict
  the outcomes of each measurement chronologically. The mean of the
  outcomes is calculated, as well as the standard deviation. In addition to
  these two items the Upper and Lower Control Limits are calculated by
  adding or subtracting three times the standard deviation from the mean.
  If the process is without trends and statistically under control, no signals
  will show up. A process that is not under control is unpredictable; the
  process capability analysis can still be performed but is of little predictive
  value.
- **Distribution Analysis** - here the shape of distribution (eg normal or
  Weibull) is determined. This is important as it sets the standard for the
  type of Process Capability Analysis.
- **Process Capability Analysis** - here the quality of the process, as it
  is now and will be in the future, is set against the Specification limits
  determined by your customer. If 99.99966% of all outcomes fall within
  the upper and lower specification limits, your process performs at a Six
  Sigma level. If it is not, it is yet to be improved.

Now that the process capability is known, more accurate predictions can be made about the goals of the project. Typically, the process is improved by 80%. The project goal should consist of only two things:

- **Mean** - a new mean (goals) for the Int CTQ must be formulated. This will depict the centre of output values of the improved process.
- **Variance** - a new level of variance for the Int CTQ must be set in order to determine how the future process may fluctuate in order to stay within specification limits at all times.

The difference between the old mean and variations and the new values will be the ultimate savings prediction of the project.

As the differences between the current and the target mean and variation are known, a list can be composed where possible influence factors on that Int CTQ are summed up. It is important to work the system like a funnel: write down as many potential influence factors as you can, you will reject most of them later on and identify just a few that really matter. Useful tools for this part of the project are:

- Exploratory data analysis
- Pareto charts
- CTQ-flow downs
- Failure Mode and Effect Analysis (FMEA)
- Brainstorming
- Fishbone Diagram
- Priority Matrix
- Root Cause Analysis

These tools will be discussed in Chapter 4 and Appendix C. Some of these tools can be automated using quality management applications for IT management.

We end with a long list of potential influence factors which will be checked on significance for Int CTQ.

## 2.4.4 DMAIC: **Improve (4)**

The list of potential influence factors on the Int CTQ needs to be checked systematically through hypothesis testing. For each potential influence factor, a set of hypotheses will be formulated. The standard way to do this is by setting a conservative (H0) hypothesis which states there is no significant connection between the potential influence factor and the Int CTQ, and an alternative (H1) hypothesis that states there is a significant connection between the potential influence factor and the Int CTQ.

After all the factors have been tested against the Int CTQ, a number of potential influence factors will prove to be important predictors for the behavior of the Int CTQ. The majority, however, will not have a significant connection. Thus, we differentiate the 'vital few' from the 'trivial many'. The insignificant potential influence factors will now be discarded from the project.

Given the limited list of vital influence factors, a mathematical equation must now be formulated to model their effect on the Int CTQ. There are a number of methods for this:

- **Regression analysis** - this method models the relationship between one vital influence factor and the Int CTQ. It is also possible to model multiple vital influence factors. It is most useful when good quality historical data is available.
- **Design of Experiment (DoE)** - here, a number of vital influence factors can be modeled for their effect on the Int CTQ through systematic variation among them. Contrary to regression analysis, you can establish causation with DoE. This method is also very useful when data is not readily available and time is limited.
- **General Linear Model (GLM)** - should one or more of the vital influence factors be of a discrete order, whereas the others are of continuous order, a GLM can still model a transfer function by selecting factors for the discrete vital influences and co-variates for the continuous

ones. The interpretation of the model also allows for an interaction effect.

The result of all these efforts is a clear-cut transfer function which looks like this:

$$Ext\ CTQ = Int\ CTQ = f(X1;\ X2;\ X3;\ Xn\text{-}1;\ Xn)$$

Every X is a vital influence factor and the 'f' denotes the function in which it influences Int CTQ. This is a complex way of describing the way in which each influence factor (X) affects the Int CTQ. In addition to each important X influencing Int CTQ, different influence factors (Xs) can also influence one another. It is therefore important to assess the interaction between the Xs and per X on the Int CTQ. This is called a transfer function.

Since the optimal Int CTQ mean and variation are known from the process capability analysis, for each vital influence factor the following can be calculated from the transfer function:
• optimal mean of X to yield optimal mean for Int CTQ
• maximum of allowed variation in X to stay within the LSL and USL for Int CTQ

For each vital influence factor X, this yields the optimal setting of its mean and the maximum range of its variation corresponding to optimum value of Int CTQ.

All that needs to be done now is to control all vital influence factors within their Upper and Lower Tolerance Limits. These control measures are easy to identify and constitute the true improvements of the process.

This is also where Six Sigma shows its added value. Instead of merely measuring the outcomes, the influence factors on that outcome have been identified and controlled. This provides the means to manage, adapt and improve the process as required.

## 2.4.5 DMAIC: Control (5)

In order to keep the improved process under control, a measurement system has to be constructed to measure the Int CTQ as well as the vital influence factors that predict it.

The same issues apply here as pointed out in the Measure phase. A number of tools are available to increase control over the new process:

- **OCAP (Out of Control Action Plan)** - this is a decision tree that lists the most common problems and their most effective remedies.
- **Poka Yoke or Mistake Proofing** - Mistake Proofing reduces the chances for mistakes by virtue of the design of the process. It is oriented to finding and correcting problems (faults) as close to the source as possible because finding and correcting defects caused by errors costs more and more as the product or item flows through a process. For example: your car with automatic gearbox will not shift into 'drive' if the brakes are not applied.
- **Control loops and Control charts** - these indicate whether the Int CTQ and all its vital influence factors are still within limits or not. As soon as any of these vital influence factors steps out of its tolerance limits, it shows up in the control loop and on the control chart. Action can be taken accordingly, for example through an OCAP.

Now that the new process is accurately measured and controlled, it can be assessed by a new process capability analysis. This analysis is the same as the one explained in section 2.4.3 in this chapter and yields the number of observations that will fall within specification limits on both the long and the short term. Financial benefits can now be measured, calculated and signed off by the controller. The final act is to hand over the improved process to daily operations and the quality assurance department.

While handing the improved process over to daily operations, it is extremely important to communicate the new routines to them as well as possible. The richer the documentation and management support is in this phase, the better Supervisors or Co-ordinators (operational staff) will be able to control the new process themselves. The better the Six Sigma team analyzed and improved the new process, the better relevant situations will be documented in detail and have accurate instructions on how to solve them. This will create an improved process, working according to customer specifications (or exceeding their expectation) for a long time.

### 2.4.6 Report

Documenting the processes and results of Six Sigma projects is an important step for lessons learned and handover (if any). Many Six Sigma projects will include *Reporting as part of the Control* phase. The daily capability of the improved process needs to be reported if the improvements are meant to last. This reporting generally consists of two methods:

- reporting on the Int CTQ of the process and its vital influence factors
- reporting on the results in terms of financial benefits and increase in customer satisfaction

The better the match between the method of reporting and the goals of the company, the better the process will be managed over time.

A final important consideration on reporting is to share and claim successes that have been achieved by performing the Six Sigma project. Communicating this success is vital to validating the value of Six Sigma in the organization and in maintaining momentum for continual improvement. Further such success may well generate spin-offs or fuel other projects under consideration.

# 3 Combining Six Sigma and ITIL

## 3.1 What is ITIL?

ITIL (Information Technology Infrastructure Library) offers a common framework for all activities of the IT department as part of service provisioning based on the IT infrastructure.[1] These activities are divided into processes supporting five principle elements (see Figure 3.1); Business Perspective, Managing Applications, Delivery of IT Services, Support of IT Services, and Manage the Infrastructure. Together, they provide an effective framework to make IT Service Management more mature. Each of these processes covers one or more tasks of the IT department, such as service development, infrastructure management, and supplying and supporting the services.

ITIL is not a methodology and it is not prescriptive. It simply describes and explains processes and their relationships between the activities that are necessary to implement Service Management. It is flexible and adaptable enough that organizations can apply areas of ITIL that best meet their needs.

The framework was developed in the 1980s when the British Government asked the CCTA (Central Computer and Telecommunications Agency, now the Office of Government Commerce, OGC) to develop an approach for efficient and cost-effective use of IT resources. Sensitive to the escalating costs of IT they sought a means to establish best practice processes for IT.

---

1 This pocket guide is based on ITIL version 2 and prior. ITIL version 3 is expected in 2007. This will follow a lifecycle model that includes Service Strategies, Service Design, Service Transition and Service Operation and Continual Service Improvement.

CCTA collected information on how various organizations addressed Service Management, analyzed this and filtered those issues that would prove useful to CCTA and to IT customers in UK central government. Other organizations found the guide applicable to industries outside the government. By the mid-1990s, ITIL was recognized as the de facto standard for IT Service Management. A review of the ITIL framework is underway to better represent best practices in light of recent developments in technology.

The ITIL framework consists of five principal elements, each of which has interfaces and overlaps with each of the other four. The elements are:
• Business Perspective
• Managing Applications
• Deliver IT Services
• Support IT Services
• Manage the Infrastructure

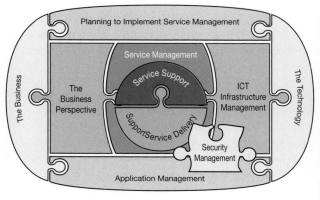

Figure 3.1 The ITIL publication framework (Based on: OGC source)

Figure 3.1 shows the overall environment and structure within which the modules were produced. It illustrates the relationship that each of the modules has with the business and the technology. From the diagram it can be seen how the Business Perspective module is more closely aligned to the business and the ICT Infrastructure Management module is more closely aligned with the technology itself. The Service Delivery and Service Support modules provide the heart of the process framework:

1. **Service Delivery** - consists of the processes required for the planning and delivery of quality IT services:

    - *Capacity Management* - ensures that the customer's present and future needs are always provided with sufficient capacity of IT resources against justified costs, in the right place and at the right time.

    - *Financial Management for IT Services* - provides insight in the actual costs of services, thus allowing IT to deliver services in a cost-effective manner and provide information for fact-based decisions relating to services value to the enterprise.

    - *Availability Management* - concerns design, implementation, measurement and management of IT services to ensure that stated availability requirements are met.

    - *Service Level Management* - aims to clarify agreements with the customer about the type and quality of IT services to be delivered, and to implement, control, analyze, monitor and improve the services addressed in the agreements.

    - *IT Service Continuity Management* - supports the overall Business Continuity Management process by ensuring that IT Services can be recovered within required and agreed business timescales.

2. **Service Support** – consists of the processes required for day-to day support and maintenance activities in order to provide IT services:

    - *Service Desk* (actually not a process, but a function within an organization) - supports the agreed IT service as stated in the SLA by serving as a single point of contact for the user and customer so the IT organization is accessible and support issues are addressed effectively and in line with business priorities.

- *Incident Management* - restores normal IT service operation as quickly as possible, and minimizes the adverse impact on business operations, thus assuring the best possible levels of service quality and availability as agreed in the Service Level Agreements.
- *Problem Management* - minimizes the adverse impact of incidents and problems on the business, caused by errors within the IT Infrastructure and prevents recurrence of incidents related to these errors.
- *Configuration Management* - provides a logical model of the infrastructure or a specific service by identifying, controlling, maintaining and verifying the versions of Configuration Items (CIs) in existence.
- *Change Management* - ensures that standardized methods and procedures are used for efficient and prompt handling of all changes, in order to minimize the impact of change-related incidents upon service quality, with minimal or accepted risks for the IT service provision.
- *Release Management* - plans and controls releases of software and hardware Design and implement efficient procedures for distribution and installation to protect the live environment and its services.

3. **Security Management** – is concerned with planning and managing a defined security level for IT services.

4. **ICT Infrastructure Management (ICT IM)** - includes the identification of business requirements, the testing, installation, deployment, and ongoing operation and optimization of the ICT components and IT services.

5. **Application Management** - describes how to manage applications from the initial business need, through all stages in the application lifecycle, including retirement.

6. **The Business Perspective** - helps IT personnel understand how they can contribute to the business objectives and how their roles and services can be better aligned and exploited to maximize that contribution.

7. **Planning to Implement Service Management** – provides guidelines for planning, implementing and improving Service Management processes within an organization.

## 3.2 Why Six Sigma complements ITIL

> *"By year-end 2010, ITIL, Six Sigma and CobiT will become the de facto process, quality and governance frameworks utilized by IT operational groups."*[2]

Delivering quality IT services to the business continues to be a priority for IT executives. Organizations have looked to combine ITIL and other quality methodologies such as Six Sigma to address performance requirements. Six Sigma and ITIL are often promoted as complementary - the two principles are both aimed to increase quality and satisfy customers. So why does Six Sigma complement ITIL?

ITIL is the worldwide de facto standard framework for IT Service Management and is a framework based on a set of best practices to deliver and support IT services. However, without mechanisms to quantify baseline quality levels, and measure quality improvement, ITIL can benefit from Six Sigma to understand: Where are the defects within the ITIL processes? What is the Cost of Poor Quality (COPQ) to the business? What processes are Critical to Quality (CTQ) and are therefore most worthy to improve? What is the relative improvement of quality levels? While ITIL benefits from Six Sigma, Six Sigma is more effective when a process is already in place which ITIL provides.

Six Sigma is a proven quality methodology that is increasingly gaining momentum in various industry sectors. Like many quality management processes, it uses statistical techniques to continuously measure, analyze

---

2  "Leveraging ITIL, and Other Process/Quality/Governance for IT Operational Success." Gartner, Ed Holub, Gartner Data Center Conference, December 2005.

and improve quality which can be applied to any discipline, including service management processes based on ITIL. Tools from IT Management vendors now automate Six Sigma techniques to analyze the plethora of data; leading vendors with this advanced capabilities include Proxima Technology, BMC, IBM and HP. Six Sigma differs from most quality management processes in that it focuses quality improvement activities on those business processes that really matter to the business. That is, it is not *quality for quality's sake*, it is quality where it matters. The measure of 'where it matters' is measured purely in cost terms. This more pragmatic approach is one of the key reasons for Six Sigma's popularity.

The combination of Six Sigma and ITIL provide the most comprehensive quality and service management solution, with a focus on delivering value to the business.

Forrester Research, an independent technology research firm, comments:

> *"For companies already in ITIL implementation, Forrester recommends enhancements to the measurement system through the use of Six Sigma."*[3]

The exact reasons why Six Sigma and ITIL complement each other can be divided into four categories:

- **Aligning IT with the business**
  - Six Sigma provides a non-subjective mechanism to communicate service quality improvement to business people, in business terms.
  - Six Sigma helps increase IT credibility as it has strong mindshare with C-Level business executives.
  - Six Sigma helps mitigate IT operational risks and supports compliance initiatives.
  - Six Sigma brings a sense of priority to service improvement initiatives based on business criticality.

---

3  "Beyond ITIL: Despite Hype Full Implementations Are the Exception", Giga Research (Forrester), Thomas Mendel, October 2003.

- **Measuring quality of service**
  - Six Sigma supports the use of predictive models which provide a proactive approach to process improvement.
  - ITIL advocates thinking in terms of services, something that is not a particular focus of Six Sigma.
  - Six Sigma can contribute to making visible which services add the most value to the business and therefore should have a higher priority.
  - ITIL lacks a quality measurement, analysis and a detailed continual process improvement methodology. Six Sigma provides this to ITIL.
  - Six Sigma facilitates the elimination of defects (in terms of reducing the COPQ) in processes supporting CTQ business functions.
  - Six Sigma drives better metrics.
- **Adaptability**
  - Six Sigma is adaptable to changing business and customer demand.
  - Six Sigma is not complex; it is based on commonly accepted statistical principles that business and technical personnel easily comprehend.
- **Market trends**
  - Six Sigma is gaining momentum in the ITIL community and the recognized 'pragmatic business-driven approach' to IT service quality improvement.
  - Six Sigma has proven to be successful using established statistical tools and techniques.

## 3.2.1 Aligning IT with the business

Six Sigma techniques clarify the process of aligning IT with the business by reinforcing business concepts within IT, thus helping IT organizations think and run IT like a business.

For example, Six Sigma concepts and techniques such as COPQ, Defects/Opportunities, CTQ, Process Sigma Value and Voice of the Customer (VOC), among others, help IT articulate clearly in a common language (profit/loss, cost of poor quality, cost/benefit analysis, etc.) to the business people.

Effective communication using a language everyone understands helps the organization achieve its strategic goals. Moreover, this applies to the teams directly involved with improvement projects, ensuring that responsibilities and tasks are communicated and no accountability issues arise.

ITIL is rapidly gaining the mindshare of top IT executives globally, but it does not yet have the attention of business executives to the same extent as Six Sigma. Six Sigma is widely regarded as a business improvement methodology. IT organizations successfully using Six Sigma will gain credibility of the business and will be in a better position to prove their business value.

Furthermore, organizations looking into risk management and compliance (Basel II, Sarbanes-Oxley, etc.) can use Six Sigma as 'value-add' to ITIL and governance frameworks like Control Objectives for Information and Related Technology (known as CobiT). It provides a detailed continual process improvement-approach to risk management and auditing activities by treating them like a process.

Thus, organizations can predict different scenarios, helping them to manage and avoid risk. Six Sigma-based scenarios result in different options, so that management can decide what risk level they are willing to take. This is a sound decision base that no other methodology will deliver. If parameters change during the implementation of a process, Six Sigma will allow you to predict the effects because of the model-based approach. Thus, the main advantages are:

- adding a level of predictability to IT services
- providing an opportunity to assess the business impact of a change to an implementation

This reduces the risk of surprise which is exactly what business and IT desire.

## 3.2.2 Measuring quality of service

ITIL on its own indicates the quality of service, but it requires a
measurement and quality discipline like Six Sigma. Six Sigma, on the
other hand, is best used when there is a process to improve, this is
where ITIL excels. To illustrate using Change Management: Change
Management can be implemented following the ITIL guidelines. This in
itself does not guarantee the quality of implementation or help improve
the implementation of the process over time. ITIL does provide some
suggestions for metrics to be used by Change Management, but is very
brief in explaining how to use them in practice.

Six Sigma complements ITIL by providing a mechanism to measure the
quality of the Change Management process output. Further, Six Sigma
provides guidance in continual improvement to ensure performance within
specification limits.

Moreover, Six Sigma helps drive better metrics overall because it brings
business context into IT. Six Sigma quantifies benefits and quality
improvements that can help IT increase their credibility to the business.
Examples of metrics that can be used are:
• process sigma value for quality of service (including yield, and defect/
  opportunity counts like DPMO)
• COPQ in monetary value tied to CTQ service degradation or failure (to
  show business impact)
• lost revenue
• penalty fees
• other costs associated with fixing service issues
• specification limits and control limits based on CTQ customer
  requirements to ensure client needs are met
• risk metrics such as FMEA's Risk Priority Number (RPN) to prioritize
  improvement targets
• process capability indices to gauge how close a process or service
  performance is to the specified limits

- customer perception of service through VOC to measure client satisfaction
- employee productivity (number of users, business units and locations affected due to IT outage) to show business impact, among many others

While ITIL recommends a number of metrics appropriate for the respective processes, one must consider which metrics are appropriate for the specific environment and why. Adopting a 'less is more' approach to carefully selecting metrics is recommended.

Six Sigma can help select the vital few metrics to focus on CTQ customer requirements. What is important is selecting CTQ metrics that show the business value. Monetary units are easy to understand and widely valued. Other metrics could include business impact information such as the number of users and business locations, functions, processes, applications, or customers affected.

## 3.2.3  Adaptability

Six Sigma lends itself to a competitive market where the definition of 'acceptable' changes over time. A less critical IT function may be at a four sigma value and be acceptable to customers and stakeholders, while a more critical function might require a six sigma value. While both would quantify the business impact of defects, clearly for some mission-critical or life-and-death situations targeting six sigma at 3.4 DPMO, would be intolerable.

The process sigma value is used to highlight service quality and is based on the definitions of the opportunity and defect.

For example, a Critical to Quality business service must be 100% available, except for one hour on the last Sunday of every month from 12.00 am to 1.00 am Eastern Standard Time for maintenance purposes. In this case, a time-based model is used where the total time that the service should be available is considered an opportunity and the time that the service is unavailable during that time is a defect. To illustrate, the opportunity and defect definitions for the month of September are as follows:

**Opportunities:** 43,140 minutes are the defined opportunities minus the 60 minute scheduled downtime:

[(60 minutes * 24 hours * 30 days)-60 minutes]

**Defects:** the business service was not available at any time during the 43,140 minutes of September. For example:

*Outage A*: outage lasted for 5 minutes on a Tuesday
*Outage B*: outage lasted for 10 minutes on a Thursday
*Outage C*: outage lasted for 1 minute on a Saturday

The defect total for the month of September is 16, by adding A, B, C outages. If an outage occurred during the scheduled downtime window (Sunday between 12 am EST and 1 am EST), then there would be no defects recorded.

One important aspect of the Six Sigma measure is its non-linear relationship to defect rates. You achieve a lot more in terms of reduced defects when moving from three to four sigma, than from five to six sigma. The higher the target sigma measure, the more challenging it becomes to reach perfection. Tables 3.1 and 3.2 illustrate the defect unit reduced between three to four and five to six sigma. From three to four sigma, 60,600.93 units of defects are reduced. From five to six sigma, only 229.27 defects are reduced.

| Improvement | Yield | Defects |
|---|---|---|
| 3 sigma | 93.31% | 66810.63 |
| 4 sigma | 99.65% | 6209.70 |
| Defect unit reduced | | 60600.93 |

Table 3.1 Reduction of defects from three to four sigma

| Improvement | Yield | Defects |
|---|---|---|
| 5 sigma | 99.97% | 232.67 |
| 6 sigma | 99.99% | 3.4 |
| Defect unit reduced | | 229.27 |

Table 3.2 Reduction of defects from five to six sigma

### 3.2.4 Market trends

Six Sigma is the recognized pragmatic approach to measure and improve IT service quality within the IT community. Plenty of material on the subject can now be found, such as public forums, industry research reports and analyst presentations, articles in IT trade publications (eg CIO magazines[4]), ITSMF conference presentations and so on.

Lastly, Six Sigma is a proven methodology with many publicly available books and success stories from leading corporations in the world such as General Electric, Motorola, Bank of America, Barclays, Sun Microsystems, National City Corporation and Carlson Companies.

Another point worth mentioning is ITIL and the International Standardization Organization (ISO). Six Sigma complements ISO since it can provide the hard data for process documentation and auditing purposes. With ISO 9001:2000 and its focus on measurement, analysis and improvement, Six Sigma lends itself well as the 'how to' improvement process to align with ISO. With IT operations being in an electronic universe, it is safe to say that capturing data automatically is more easily done than other business functions, therefore making the Define and Measure phases more effective and easier than manually. Moreover, the data is likely to be more accurate than manual collection.

---

4 "Six Sigma Comes to IT Targeting Perfection" Tracy Mayor, CIO, February 2, 2004.

Six Sigma for IT Management – A Pocket Guide

## 3.3 Integrating Six Sigma with ITIL: important considerations

Integrating Six Sigma and ITIL takes thought and consideration, as they differ in important respects. Six Sigma is statistical in nature while ITIL is process oriented. It is not merely a matter of combining two groups, principles and concepts and expecting the end result to be a successfully integrated framework. While these models both aim at improving organizations, the means to get there are different.

In general, four aspects should be taken into consideration:
- organizational maturity
- time versus costs versus value (Triangle Model)
- different people skill requirements
- how Six Sigma's DMAIC approach can be combined with ITIL's PDCA approach

### 3.3.1 Organizational maturity

Integrating ITIL and Six Sigma requires an organizational culture that is receptive to the principles and concepts of these two models.

When used in an IT context, the word maturity, either directly or indirectly, implies capability and alignment with the business. The effective use of a change strategy to mature an organization hinges on the current capability of the organization and the relevant processes. What tools one selects from the Six Sigma, ITIL and COBIT toolboxes is dependent upon understanding the current maturity and capability of the organization.

A mature organization consists of a culture where management is fully committed to change and innovation. An immature organization is one that is silo-based, highly political, unfocused, and manages priorities on a day-by-day basis with no roadmap of the future. An IT mentality that is purely 'technology-based' and has no understanding of what it takes to

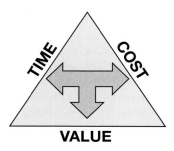

Figure 3.2 Time, cost and value

be 'business-focused' is also a feature of an immature organization. This technology or business focus dictates which tools one must use from the best practices toolkits to be effective.

### 3.3.2 Time versus cost versus value

Balancing *time, cost,* and *value* is key to successfully implementing and integrating ITIL and Six Sigma. The objective is to keep the triangle of *time, cost* and *value* equal on all three sides. If you expand one side of the triangle, the other two sides must expand as well. This will help in ensuring that the right investment is made in time and cost for the expected *value* that is to be achieved.

Let us take a look at an **example** of how one IT organization used this model to their advantage.

A company's IT department wanted to implement an ITIL-based Centralized Service Desk to support their internal customers. Unfortunately, the company would not approve the funding for implementation. The IT department was not well respected within the company and annual budgets consisted of just enough money to pay salaries and depreciation. Even after demonstrating a high return on investment, the CIO was still unsuccessful in getting Senior

Management commitment to *time* and *costs*. Determined, the CIO did not give up. He decided to take a different approach. He focused on the '*value*' perception of the current service being provided. He transformed the Service Desk into a 'Local Service Desk' with a real customer service and support mentality. The improved support changed the company's perception of the 'Helpless Desk' to a 'value-add' service. When it came to the next round of budgets, the IT department received the additional funding necessary to implement ITIL.

### 3.3.3  Different people skill requirements

Six Sigma requires an analytical skill-set. Therefore, it needs people able to work with data. These are the people who understand how to determine the capability of a process, total defects per unit, sigma value and sigma shifts.

Conversely, ITIL requires a process-oriented approach and skill-set. People having this skill-set understand operations and business activities, goals and objectives. They are typically people-focused individuals and understand people dynamics.

So what happens when you combine an analytical and detailed thinker with a process thinker? Typically, you will get a strained relationship. The process thinker will quickly run out of patience as the analytical thinker goes into great depths to understand the details. Once this happens, the Six Sigma efforts are discounted and considered too granular or unrealistic. Interestingly enough, the process thinker will often come to the same conclusion as originally identified in the Six Sigma effort but will not even know it. Unfortunately a lot of time and money can be wasted in the meantime.

Understanding people skills and the dynamics that drive them will give you an edge in managing them effectively. In this case, a cross-training program would be very effective. The Six Sigma team must understand

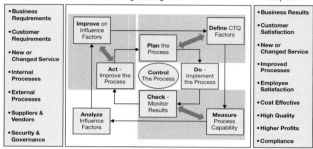

| Inputs | Six Sigma Integration Points | Outputs |
| --- | --- | --- |

Figure 3.3 Integrating PDCA with DMAIC

ITIL processes and their fluid nature. They must learn to communicate in terms that people understand. They must be able to explain that a 1.79 shift means that the process is not improving and why. The ITIL team must understand the basics of Six Sigma. An overview of Six Sigma concepts and terminology would be valuable for ITIL people. Learning to appreciate each other's skill-sets will be an enabler for a more effective and efficient team.

### 3.3.4 DMAIC vs PDCA

Understanding when, where and how to integrate Six Sigma with ITIL is also an important consideration. Let us first look at potential integration points with the *Plan, Do, Check, Act* continual improvement model.

This model is one example of how ITIL (PDCA) can be integrated with the DMAIC model of Six Sigma. Other examples would be at the process level where Six Sigma is integrated within each process such as root cause analysis for Problem Management. For this chapter, we will refer to the graph in Figure 3.3 to further demonstrate how PDCA and DMAIC can be combined.

Planning consists of clearly defining goals and objectives. Six Sigma determines these by defining what is *Critical to Quality*. By defining the external and internal CTQ parameters, a process plan can be developed that is aligned to the CTQ.

There are many Critical to Quality parameters that can be used:

- **critical to costs** – reducing costs
- **critical to quality** – improving quality
- **critical to process** – improving process capability
- **critical to time** – reducing the time to deliver

---

Let us look at the example from Chapter 2 about laptops:

**External Critical to Quality** = *Timely repair* of laptop problems
**Internal Critical to Quality** = Laptops must be repaired in under *one hour*

Using the External and Internal CTQ, it is easy to create the **objective:** *Develop and implement a process to enable the repair of laptops within one hour.*

---

Not only have the goals and objectives been clearly defined, but the scope has been defined as well – specific to laptops. A clear and concisely scoped objective in the '*planning/define*' phase will provide focus to all the proceeding steps.

However, make sure that you are measuring the right CTQ parameters – not from your perspective, but from your customer's perspective. Planning and implementing against the wrong Critical to Quality performance criteria can be detrimental.

The question that a *process thinker* should ask at this point is whether Critical to Time of laptop repairs outweighs the Critical to Quality criterion of whether the repair was completed correctly - was the laptop fixed? Is it more important to the customer that the laptop was fixed rather than being returned within an hour? If both these CTQ parameters must be met, then they must both be specified in the Planning Objective:

> *Develop and implement a process to enable **and** repair laptops within 1 hour **and ensure that the problem will not recur.***

## PDCA: Do

This phase consists of implementing the process and delivering the service that meets the objective as stated in the *planning* step. While there may not be a direct relationship with Six Sigma DMAIC, there are synergies from the standpoint of 'process mapping' the steps that need to be implemented. This will be important when Six Sigma is used to calculate process capability. The important consideration in this step is that it needs to align with ITIL best practices. Therefore, ITIL provides the guidelines.

Returning to the example on laptop repairs, an ITIL approach might be as follows.

1. **Service Level Management** defines the service and the repair times. This process ensures alignment and agreement with the customer on what the service is and what can be expected – eradicate the laptop problem within one hour.

2. **Service Desk** is the single point of contact for reporting the 'incident' (laptop error). As the single point of contact, the Service Desk provides several benefits:
   - customer interface and focus
   - ability to assess impact, urgency and priority
   - follow-up and follow-through on repair status
   - provide 'work-arounds' (loaners) and other options for the Customer while the laptop is being repaired

3. **Incident Management** provides for the recording and tracking of the 'incident' (problematic laptop). Tracking and recording the incident is important for analysis and diagnostics. This information is a key input for Six Sigma and other ITIL processes.
4. **Change Management** provides for the repair or exchange of laptops.
5. **Problem Management** allows for root cause analysis of the defective laptop and *steps to eradicate and prevent re-occurrences*, which is key to meeting the Critical to Quality criteria.

DMAIC/ PDCA: **Measure/Check**

This step monitors and measures the process against the original objectives. This is where Six Sigma can provide significant value – by measuring process capability in the short and long term. As noted, while ITIL explains 'what' needs to be measured, Six Sigma provides the tools and capabilities on 'how' to measure it.

Recall the process capability chart and the sigma shift discussed earlier about laptop repairs and the fact that while 90% of the laptops were repaired according to Service Levels, there was a long-term shift indicating that the process can get out of control. This provides clear insight on forecasting future performance capabilities and allows for proactive corrective actions. In other words, the Six Sigma analysis allows for continual improvement before service levels begin to deteriorate.

DMAIC: **Analyze**

Analyze is used by Six Sigma to drill down into factors influencing the defect. Once these factors have been identified, Six Sigma can even determine which factors have the greatest impact on the defect, thereby providing the greatest opportunity for improvement. This statistical approach to analyzing the problem is far more effective than other analysis tools or ITIL.

DMAIC/ PDCA: **Improve/Act**

Act is taking actions to continually improve process performance. To do this, you must have an idea of what to improve. Again, Six Sigma to the rescue! Six Sigma provides tools to determine which factors influence an outcome and to what degree.

In the example using laptop repairs, the average repair took 54 minutes and the long term sigma was 1.59. The *Improve* step would revert back to the process map and identify all the variables that impact this time to repair. Six Sigma 'experiments' are performed on each of these variables to determine which variable can be tuned to better control the process. Perhaps the procedure for getting the laptop to the technician needs to be improved, or perhaps the technicians do not have adequate skills to do timely repairs.

DMAIC: **Control**

The key to it all is control. It is the ability to sustain the improvements over time. This is the most challenging and is often the cause of initiatives failing. Improvements are made, but not monitored or controlled which quickly reverts back to old habits. Let us assume that training the technicians was the factor that influenced the ability to repair laptops. An outcome might be to train all the technicians, and the results will demonstrate that it indeed improved process capability.

However, the 'process thinker' should ask: what about new technicians? Will they receive the same level of training? Can the right skill-sets be maintained? What about new laptops – do the technicians need additional training to support the new technology? How can training become a step in the process (that is not forgotten or ignored)? Maintaining control takes discipline and commitment for the entire organization.

To summarize, Six Sigma DMAIC and ITIL's PDCA concepts are complementary. They can even be considered dependent on one another.

## 3.4 Integrating Six Sigma and ITIL Processes: three possible scenarios

We talked about integrating the continual improvement cycle of Six Sigma and ITIL. The appendices will provide an overview of how Six Sigma can provide value in some key ITIL processes. Each ITIL process has a major objective and specific key performance indicators (KPIs) of which Six Sigma can be used as a yardstick to measure and a goal to aim for.

This section illustrates at a high level how Six Sigma can be applied in different organizations:
1. an organization that is Six Sigma-committed and new to ITIL
2. an organization with ITIL processes established and new to Six Sigma
3. an organization that is new to both approaches

### 3.4.1 An organization that is Six Sigma-committed and new to ITIL

Many organizations are quality-committed and use Six Sigma as a quality improvement methodology company-wide. This has also meant that their IT departments use Six Sigma for their projects and are generally familiar with the tools and techniques, and when to apply them. Quality-focused organizations such as these will already have well defined processes for IT, and there is no benefit in blindly replacing every one with ITIL processes.

Here, the advantage of ITIL is that as an industry standard, there is a ready supply of people, training courses, products, consulting services and so on. In this case, where an organization embraces ITIL, they will see a reduction in costs associated with things like attrition.

Six Sigma is useful here to use real metrics to determine the IT process that is causing the highest Cost of Poor Quality and start a Six Sigma project to improve this process. At this point the relevant ITIL process can be evaluated and adapted to fit the organization in question.

For **example**, one manufacturing organization which used Six Sigma as a corporate quality methodology carried out a Six Sigma project to identify that a large number of defects were caused by their Change Management process. They used Six Sigma techniques such as the Pareto chart and Voice of the Customer along with the process sigma calculation to highlight this information and then initiate a Six Sigma project to improve the situation.

The Six Sigma project involved utilizing the DMAIC model to *define* the problem and the Cost of Poor Quality, gathering all the appropriate metrics during the *Measure* phase (for example impact on both IT and the business of failed changes), and performing detailed *analysis* of the issues with Change Management. Part of this analysis was identifying the appropriate best practices from ITIL to implement during the implementation phase. More importantly, the links between their other IT processes were also evaluated as part of this particular project to ensure that each process was not running in isolation.

One of the recommended action items in the *Improve* phase included setting up a Change Advisory Board (CAB) consisting of both IT and business professionals to ensure that changes did not disrupt CTQ business processes. Having both IT and business representatives was particularly effective during the project because this ensured that it covered all aspects (business impact and IT) of Change Management, particularly when assessing the risk and impact, defining the workflow of approvals and scheduling of changes.

Finally, in the *Control* phase the project was evaluated and its success reviewed. The team found that they had drastically reduced the number of defects caused by poor Change Management. Moreover, the improved Change Management process helped increase their confidence when audits were performed.

### 3.4.2  An organization with ITIL processes established and new to Six Sigma

This is a good position to be in because Six Sigma naturally lends itself well to improving processes that are already established. With ITIL processes established, Six Sigma provides ITIL with a structured-approach to process improvement using the DMAIC model.

Six Sigma is an especially good fit for the ITIL Service Improvement Program, and adds value to all the ITIL processes by adding a measurement and improvement methodology. However, an organization in this situation will take a broader view with Six Sigma and use this as a business process improvement initiative, and involve IT as appropriate. Typically, Six Sigma is sponsored by executive management and funds are budgeted for training and consulting services, therefore making it easier for IT to justify and adopt Six Sigma.

The Critical to Quality business processes will be identified. IT can help by measuring where IT systems add to the Cost of Poor Quality for these processes. Specific key performance indicators for each CTQ process are identified and measured, and a process sigma value derived that highlights their overall quality and gives a foundation to start improving those systems that are not performing adequately.

For **example,** consider an IT organization in a major bank that has identified ten CTQ business processes. Instead of focusing inwardly at IT processes, this particular organization focused on services supporting those ten business processes (*define*).

For each of the critical banking services that IT delivered, appropriate metrics were determined and collected, and a process sigma value was calculated for each business service (*measure*).

Also part of the project was to help IT start thinking in terms of delivering service to their customers instead of managing IT systems and applications. Thinking in terms of services is something ITIL provides and Six Sigma does not. Six Sigma can contribute to making visible which services add the most value to the business and therefore should have a higher priority.

This *analysis* highlighted a particular service for the Funds Transfer process due to its considerably low sigma value compared to the others. A process map was created to show the underlying IT services and components that make up the Funds Transfer process. The Service Model in their existing Business Service Management software was used to provide input for the process map.

Some of the techniques used during the project included VOC interviews and surveys to ensure the resulting improvements would meet the customer's requirements. A Pareto chart was used to highlight the recurring defects within the Funds Transfer system. The *Improve* phase included enhancing the application performance and adjusting the key performance indicator (KPI) thresholds in their Service Level Management product. To sustain their improved application performance and new service levels, control charts were implemented.

### 3.4.3  An organization new to Six Sigma and ITIL

If an organization is new to both ITIL and Six Sigma, then it is recommended to progress one step at a time. Six Sigma is typically a CEO top-down initiative, the benefit here is that 'having a process to improve' can be the justification for ITIL.

'Big bang' type implementations of these frameworks are rarely a success in the real world; rather, small iterative improvement steps and staying project-focused provide immediate benefit and help show the benefits to the rest of the organization, but also help understand where the problems are. Where to start also depends on the maturity of the IT environment; certain ITIL processes may need a higher priority than others. Maturity assessment of the IT environment is a good start. References such as the Capability Maturity Model or the IT Management Process Maturity Model are good examples to use.

One important aspect of bringing these disciplines into an organization is cultural change and resistance. Cultures in each organization are often vastly different; employee attitudes, morale, and 'the way things have always been done' may differ considerably. Much consideration needs to go into how these two disciplines will affect the employees.

Six Sigma champions and executives responsible for ITIL will need to plan carefully for the new procedures, and training, taking all of these issues into account in order to ensure that the transition is smooth. Cultural change is a particularly sensitive issue in organizations that have not previously used and seen the benefits from processes such as ITIL and Six Sigma.

The suggested approach in this situation is to start first with introducing the basic ITIL Service Support processes to stabilize the environment. It is not necessary to fully implement each process; rather, start with the basics and work towards a process that fits into the business requirements.

---

For **example,** a leading check clearing organization was rated 'Chaotic' based on the Capability Maturity Model. The IT department often relied on their customers or users to alert them of issues, processes were not established, the time and people involved to fix problems was excessive, and problem resolution was conducted on an ad hoc basis. The recommended solution in this instance was to first understand the Service Level Agreements, implement appropriate Incident Management, Problem Management and Change Management before bringing in Six Sigma. Six Sigma can then be used to highlight further candidates for improvement.

---

## 3.5 Summary

IT now plays a vital function in enabling business success, and in every industry today, IT is the business and the business is IT. The increasing need for standard processes and quality improvement methodologies such as ITIL and Six Sigma prove to be effective for IT to target service excellence.

ITIL's process-driven approach lacks a quality process improvement model like Six Sigma. And Six Sigma complements ITIL by providing the measurement and process improvement structure. They share a common theme, their focus on customers and quality of service.

So why does Six Sigma complement ITIL? Six Sigma:
- assists in aligning IT with the business
- measures, analyzes and improves service quality
- adapts to each IT environment and changing business and client requirements
- is the recognized 'pragmatic business-driven approach'
- allows Corporate Executives to compare quality levels in radically different corporate functions, such as IT service quality vs. sales and marketing

Before starting the integration of Six Sigma and ITIL, it is necessary to consider the IT maturity of your organization, and the amount of time and cost the integration is likely to take. You should also convince senior management to 'buy in'. Try to make them fully aware they need to be committed and stay committed to continually improving the organization's processes.

After considering these aspects, be aware of the different group of skills; Six Sigma ('data people') and ITIL ('process thinkers'). By acknowledging these differences and allowing these different kinds of people to work together for a while, they should start to complement each other instead of obstruct each other.

> *"Through 2010, Six Sigma will become the leading quality improvement framework for IT operational groups, although less than 10 percent will attempt to manage defects to <3.4/million."[5]*

The combination of ITIL and Six Sigma is particularly effective because both rely on industry standard tools and techniques. The ITIL best practices are tried and tested ways of running an efficient IT operation, and Six Sigma utilizes proven statistical techniques, many of which were in common use before the advent of Six Sigma. This ensures that there is a vast pool of IT professionals who either already know how to apply these disciplines, or are able to easily build upon existing knowledge with basic training.

In summary, ITIL brings the best practices to IT Service Management and Six Sigma provides the quality methodology to ensure that the processes are being followed and that quality is constantly being measured, reviewed and improved.

---

5 "Leveraging ITIL, and Other Process/Quality/Governance for IT Operational Success.", Gartner, Ed Holub, Gartner Data Center Conference, December 2005.

# 4 A Six Sigma approach to IT process improvement

This chapter aims to explain how Six Sigma can be used to improve IT processes, using the following Six Sigma connections:

1. **Metric** – to establish the importance of linking business requirements to information criteria (Critical to Quality/CTQ), followed by establishing Key Goal Indicators (KGIs) representing these CTQs and identify the Key Performance Indicators (KPIs) influencing the KGIs. The definition of defects can be derived from the metrics generated out of KGI and KPI data.

2. **Methodology** - the IT Process improvement approach will be structured in the DMAIC format (Tables 4.1-4.11).

3. **Philosophy** - the objective of IT process improvement is to become more customer oriented by better aligning the IT service to the business services. The variation in the IT services levels would be seen directly as variation in the business service levels. Non-conformance to required levels of information criteria of IT services would directly reflect increases in the cost of doing business. All improvement initiatives should be linked to external business triggers, and be enabled by defect reduction (depending on how one defines 'defect'). It should be possible to link all improvement initiatives to Profit/Loss.

The questions of why, what, when and how to pursue (continual) IT process improvement using Six Sigma will be answered. By the end of the chapter we will have covered the following aspects on IT process improvement:

- the role of IT processes in improving Business Services
- what is IT process improvement
- why should we consider IT process improvement

- when should we consider IT process improvement
- introduction to IT process improvement approach
- the Six Sigma approach to IT process improvement
- different phases of IT process improvement projects:
  - Recognize the future state
  - Transform to future state
  - Sustain the future state
- managing an IT process improvement project
- introduction to IT process mapping

## 4.1   IT processes in improving business services

The need to manage information is universal across the vertical and horizontal dimensions of the industry. It is the use of information technology to enable critical business processes that allow the enterprise to make its business services better, faster and cheaper.

The need to improve business services is driven by business triggers, coming from the business environment. This in turn drives the need to improve business processes and hence the underlying IT services enabling these business processes.

Similarly, new developments in information technology (technology triggers) drive the business managers to improve their business processes to either enhance the service levels of existing service or create new business services.

Thus, improvement in business services requires improvement in the IT processes, and improvement in IT processes should enable business service improvement. In simple customer terms, improvement means making business services better, faster and cheaper. However, to handle an IT process improvement project we need to be more specific about what improvement means and how to measure improvement in quantitative terms.

To satisfy business objectives, information needs to conform to certain control criteria, which we shall refer to as business requirements for information, or *information criteria*. The information criteria will be the catalyst to convert the business objectives to IT process objectives.

Information criteria based on the broader quality, fiduciary and security requirements, along with well defined key goal and performance metrics, ensure that the IT process improvement effort is well aligned with the business objectives.

We shall borrow the philosophy and terms from best practices such as COBIT, ITIL, PMBoK and PRINCE2 in discussing our approach to business-aligned IT process improvement.

## 4.2 The IT process improvement approach

> *IT process improvement is a customer-focused, systematic, data-driven paradigm to recognize, transform and sustain a desired future state by achieving IT control objectives.*

Let us further elaborate on the above definition:

- improvement as perceived by customers through the voice of the **customer**, both internal and external
- improvement is not achieved accidently, by chance. Adopting a well defined **systematic** approach towards recognizing, transforming and sustaining the desired future state is required. In such a Controlled Process Approach (CPA), the first thing to be established is a clear goal and an Upper and Lower Specification Limit for this goal (USL and LSL)
- commitment to improvement comes from a positive **paradigm** (mindset) to change towards a better way of doing things. It involves the ability to see the future state, as will be explained, and the willingness to commit to the journey of change

- **recognize** improvement opportunities by regularly comparing the current state with the requirement derived after considering the business and technology triggers. This could be done for example by Balanced Scorecard (BSC) or benchmarking
- **sustain** the future state benefits demonstrated and achieved through transformation. This involves organizational Change Management and Quality Assurance
- the **future state** represents the requirement to make services better, faster and cheaper. A future state should be represented in terms of:
  - business service metrics like revenue, cost, profit or
  - IT service information criteria metric or
  - IT process KGI / KPI metric
  - **IT control objective** is a statement of the desired result or purpose to be achieved by implementing control procedures in a particular IT activity

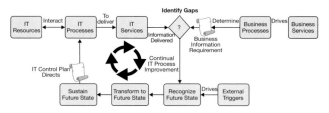

Figure 4.1 Business driven IT process improvement

A holistic approach (Figure 4.1) towards IT process improvement requires techniques to:

- **identify improvement objectives (Recognize Future State):** the Recognition phase identifies the IT process improvement projects that need to be carried out. The current state is compared with the current requirement to identify gaps. The business triggers and the technology triggers are evaluated to identify need or potential for improvement

- *input* - gaps in current state, external triggers (business and technology)
- *output* - IT process improvement project charter
- **implement improvement objectives (Transforming to Future State):** the *Transformation* phase carries out the transition from the current state to the future state, by managing the relationships between the IT process variables, activities and controls
  - *Input* - IT process improvement project charter
  - *Output* - improvement solution
- **adopt and retain improvement benefits (Sustain the Future State):** the *Sustain* phase designs and executes a control plan to ensure adoption and retention of the IT control effectiveness. The potential benefits projected through the IT process improvement project are actually realized during this phase
  - *input* - improvement solution
  - *output* - IT control plan
- **manage the 'improvement projects' (Achieve objectives within the constraint of time, cost and quality):** an IT process improvement initiative is a project and hence needs to be managed using project management techniques. These techniques reduce the project risks and increase the probability of success

Those parts of IT process improvement can be embedded in Six Sigma's DMAIC guidelines, as section 4.3 explains.

## 4.2.1  IT process improvement terminology

Much-used terms in IT process improvement are:
- **Key Goal Indicators (KGIs)** - define measures that tell management whether an IT process has achieved its business requirements (*goals*), usually expressed in terms of information criteria:
  - availability of information needed to support the business needs
  - absence of integrity and confidentiality risks

    – cost-efficiency of processes and operations

    – confirmation of reliability, effectiveness and compliance

In Six Sigma terms, a KGI can be explained as the external CTQ.

- **Key Performance Indicators (KPIs)** - define measures to determine how well the IT process is performing in enabling the goal to be reached. They are lead indicators for determining whether a goal is likely to be reached or not. The KPI is Six Sigma's internal CTQ.
- **IT control** - the policies, procedures, practices and organizational structures designed to provide reasonable assurance that business objectives will be achieved. Also, control should prevent undesired events or at least detect them after occuring and then correct them. This embodies Six Sigma's DMAIC Control phase.
- **IT control objective** - a statement of the desired result or purpose to be achieved by implementing control procedures in a particular IT activity.

## 4.2.2 Why consider IT process improvement

Improvement helps to make existing systems more efficient and effective. It is the tool that helps to realize the future state, representing the system goals and objectives. A successful IT process improvement project can have the following broad outcomes:

- have a positive impact on IT service by increasing one or more business information criteria like effectiveness, efficiency, integrity, confidentiality, availability, reliability and compliance (COBIT)
- have a positive impact on IT services by reducing costs, incidents, response times, restoration times and repair times

Figure 4.2 shows improvements in IT services will lead to improvement in business services, being the ultimate goal of an enterprise.

## 4.2.3 When to consider IT process improvement

The desire to undertake IT process improvement could emerge from two reasons:

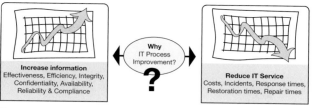

Figure 4.2 Benefits of IT process improvement

- **reactive mode:**
  - *gaps in current state* - the current state IT processes are not able to deliver IT services meeting business information requirements
  - *benchmarking* - competitive pressure or need to operate at levels set per industry benchmarks
- **proactive mode:**
  - *retain leadership position* - enterprises using IT as a strategic enabler to create new services could look at improvement to retain their leadership position through IT process improvement
  - *achieve entitlement or capability limits* - enterprises that pride themselves on their high level of operational efficiency could improve their yield by achieving process entitlement[1] or capability limits through IT process improvement

## 4.3 The Six Sigma approach to IT process improvement

If we call the outcome of a process '**Y**', and see it as the result of different in(ter)dependent process variables called '**X**', we can define the function to determine the process outcome as follows:

---

1 Existing IT processes can be improved to reach new eligible limits or heights by adopting a continual improvement approach. For example, an existing change management process which doesn't have a multi function representation would significantly benefit by the introduction of a multifunctional CAB. The change management process that is implemented within a function is useful, but would not be able to realize the true potential or entitlement of the change management process, unless it brings in representation from other dependent functions. Continual IT process improvement by adding new controls or strengthening exisiting controls would help the IT Process to achieve new entitlement or capability limits.

> **Y = f (X1 X2 X3 X4 Xn)**
> With process outcome **Y** being a dependent variable that is a function
> of the independent process variables (**X**) that influence the outcome of
> variable Y and each other.

For IT process improvement the challenges are in:

- **identifying KGIs (external CTQs)** that indicate the outcome (**Y**),
  representing the information characteristics (effectiveness, efficiency,
  confidentiality, integrity, availability, compliance and reliability) of IT
  services
- **identifying KPIs (internal CTQs)** that are influenced by the
  in(ter)dependent process variables X's (IT controls). From these KPIs,
  the KGIs can be derived
- **identifying the IT controls (the Xs)** and sub-controls that directly
  influence the KPIs
- selecting the **appropriate maturity level** for the IT controls
- **validating** that the KGI/KPI target values can be achieved through
  selected process controls (for example the solution quality)
- ensuring **adoption and maintenance** of the desired control solution (for
  example change acceptance)

In this way, the function becomes:

> $$KGI = F(KPIs) = F \ (IT \ controls, \ to \ n)$$

## 4.4 Six Sigma in the IT process improvement phases

The first IT process improvement phase consists of recognizing the desired
*Future State*, determined by business- as well as technology - requirements
(*triggers*). This phase constitutes basically the same as Six Sigma's *define*
phase.

After the desired future state has been agreed upon, the transformation
to this state begins, being the second phase. This is always a matter of
determining where the organization is now, called *Measure and Analyze* in
Six Sigma, and afterwards making a plan to get there. This is followed by
the *Improve* phase in Six Sigma.

After the desired future state has been attained, an organization needs to
sustain this state, or in Six Sigma terms, *Control* it. This is the third phase
of IT process improvement. Figure 4.3 shows how Six Sigma's DMAIC can
be embedded in IT process improvement.

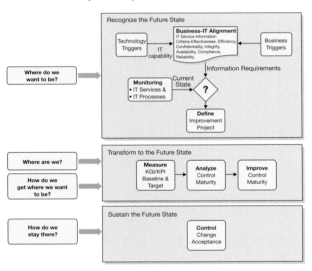

Figure 4.3 IT process improvement phases (source: CobiT/ISACA)

Table 4.1 provides a representative listing of Six Sigma tools that can
be used while embarking on an IT process improvement initiative. The
activity numbers in the table heading refer to the tasks and activities
highlighted in Tables 4.2 up to 4.11.

| SN | Six Sigma tools | Relevance for IT Process improvement | Phase and activity number | | | | | | |
|---|---|---|---|---|---|---|---|---|---|
| | Six Sigma phase | | D | M | | A | | I | C |
| | Activity number | | 1 | 2 | 3 | 4 | 5 | 6 | 7 |
| 1. | Affinity Diagram | Establish improvement scope. | | | | | | | ■ |
| 2. | Project Charter | Articulate improvement objective, resources available, benefits and timeline. | ■ | | | | | | |
| 3. | Run Charts | Observe, detect and demonstrate KGI / KPI variation. | | ■ | | | | | |
| 4. | VOC / VOB | Capture requirements / expectations / issues as perceived by customer / business. | | ■ | | | | | |
| 5. | CTQ tree | Derive information requirements (CTQs) from business requirements, issues or VOC. | | | ■ | | | | |
| 6. | Kano Model | Categorize requirements into must have, better to have and delighters. | | | | ■ | | | |
| 7. | Pareto Chart | Organize data and prioritize issues. | | | ■ | ■ | | | |
| 8. | SIPOC | Understand the process elements and their interactions. | | ■ | | | | | |
| 9. | Toll gate review | Track and ensure that desired improvement results are actually achieved. | ■ | | ■ | | ■ | ■ | |
| 10. | Y=f(X) | Differentiate and establish relationship between the CTQ or process outcome (information criteria and KGI) and the factors(controls and KPI) impacting the outcome. | | | | | ■ | ■ | |
| 11. | Brainstorming | Creatively generate lots of ideas . | | | | | ■ | | |
| 12. | Hypothesis testing | To differentiate the 'vital few' from the 'trivial many'. The insignificant potential influence factors can thus be discarded from the project (see Chapter 2). | | | | | ■ | | |

| # | Tool | Description |
|---|------|-------------|
| 13. | Modeling | The effects of the limited list of vital influence factors must now be modeled on the Int CTQ. This can be done by for example Regression analysis, Design of Experiment, or a General Linear Model. A mathematical equation can thus be formulated to model their effect on the Int CTQ (see next tool). |
| 14. | MSA | Select measurement plan for KGI / KPI. |
| 15. | Cause and effect diagram | Enables team to identify, explore, dig deeper and graphically display the causes related to a problem. |
| 16. | Activity diagram | Track execution of action plans. |
| 17. | FMEA | Risk Management. |
| 18. | Involvement Matrix | Describe who should be involved and for what to facilitate change management. |
| 19. | PDCA | Continual improvement approach to make processes better and better. |
| 20. | Process Management Chart | Documents PDCA improvement plan. Provides guidance on how to act if something goes wrong. Serves as a self audit tool. |

■ Tool usage highly recommended

▨ Tool may be used to facilitate activity

Table 4.1 Six Sigma tools that can be used for IT Process Improvement

## 4.4.1 Phase 1 - Recognize the Future State

DMAIC: **Define**

Table 4.2 shows how the project goals can be defined.

| Step | Activity number | Activity description | Input | Output |
|------|-----------------|---------------------|-------|--------|
| **Define** | 1 | Assess the Current State metric against the Business Information Requirement to identify gaps. | Business Information Requirement for each IT Service. Current State Metric for IT services & IT processes. | Improvement Project Charter. |
| | | Formulate the Improvement Project Charter on discovery of gaps that warrant an improvement project. | | |

Table 4.2 Defining the project goals

The project definition charter should articulate the following:

- **information requirement** - should be stated in terms of the seven information criteria for example *effectiveness, efficiency, confidentiality, integrity, availability, compliance* and *reliability*
- **impact due to changes/gaps** - should state the impact on the business or IT service due to not meeting the information requirement. The impact can be stated in terms of revenue, cost, usage, customer satisfaction, availability or performance
- identify the **project sponsor** and other stakeholders
- high-level **SIPOC map** (see Appendix C.24) for the current state - should identify all relevant elements of a process improvement project before the actual work begins. According to the tool's acronym, these elements are divided into *Suppliers, Input, Process, Output* and *Customers*. The tool is related to process mapping, which will be further discussed in section 4.6

- **scope** of the improvement project in terms of IT services, users, locations, specific IT service components and IT processes
- **tangible deliverable** eg change of KGI/KPI metric from _____ to _____
- **target date** for project completion

## 4.4.2 Phase 2 - Transform to the Future State

DMAIC: **Measure**

Table 4.3 shows how to get your *Measure* phase on track. Table 4.4 provides a form to document these steps. In Six Sigma, the KGI can be interpreted as the external CTQ, and the KPI as the internal CTQ.

| Step | Activity number | Activity description | Input | Output |
|------|-----------------|---------------------|-------|--------|
| **Measure** | 2 | Identify the information criteria that need improvement. | Improvement Project Charter | One separate table (Table 4.4) for each Information Criteria. |
| | | Identify the high-level controls that impact the information criteria. | | |
| | | Identify the relevant KGI/KPI corresponding to the high-level control. | | |
| | | Identify the measurement plan for the selected KGI/KPI. | | |
| | | Populate the current and target values for the selected KGI/KPI. | | |

Table 4.3 Measuring the KGIs (external CTQ) and KPIs (internal CTQ)

| High-level control objective | KGI/KPI | Measurement Plan | Current value | Target value |
|---|---|---|---|---|
| <Free Text> | <Free Text> | <Formulae> | <Numeric> | <Numeric> |

Table 4.4 Form for *Measure* step

In order to define the control objectives and the practices corresponding to your KGIs and KPIs, you could follow the walk-through scheme shown in Figure 4.4.

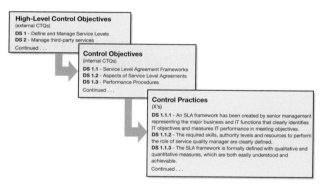

Figure 4.4 Example of high-level IT control objective, control objective and control practices (source: CobiT/ISACA)

## DMAIC: **Analyze**

Table 4.5 shows how to get your *Analyze* phase on track. Tables 4.6 and 4.7 provide forms with suggestions on how to document these steps.

| Step | Activity number | Activity description | Input | Output |
|------|-----------------|----------------------|-------|--------|
| **Analyze** | 3 | List the high-level control objectives. | One separate table (Table 4.4) for each information criteria. | Table 4.6 |
| | | List the relevant KGI/KPI. | | |
| | | Populate the target values for each KGI/KPI. | | |
| | | List the influencing control objectives against each KGI/KPI. | | |
| | | Make hypothesis test, build model to check this (check if the supposed Y's are correct). | | |
| | | List the control practices influencing the KGI/KPI against each control objective. | | |
| | | Populate the current maturity level of each control practice. | | |
| | | Populate the scope for maturity improvement for each control practice. | | |
| | | Populate the impact each control practice has on the KGI/KPI. | | |
| | 4 | List the prioritized control practices based upon scope for maturity improvement and impact on KGI/KPI. | Table 4.6 | Table 4.7 |
| | | Populate the current and target maturity levels for each control practice. | | |
| | | Estimate the resource requirement to improve the maturity to target level. | | |
| | | Assign responsibility to a process owner. | | |
| | | List the potential risks in achieving the target maturity level. | | |

Table 4.5 Analyzing the measurements

| High-level control objective | KGI/ KPI | Target value | Control objective influencing KGI/KPI | Control practices influencing KGI/KPI | Current maturity | Improvement scope | Impact on KGI/KPI |
|---|---|---|---|---|---|---|---|
| <Free text> | <Free text> | <Numeric> | <Free text> | <Free text> | <Numeric> | <H/M/L> | <H/M/L> |

Table 4.6 Form for *Analyze-3* step

| Control practices (prioritized) | Current maturity | Target maturity | Resource estimate | Process owner | Risks? |
|---|---|---|---|---|---|
| <Free text> | <Numeric> | <Numeric> | <Free text> | <Free text> | <Free text> |

Table 4.7 Form for *Analyze-4* step

While analyzing, you could use the scheme provided in Table 4.8, in order to assess the state of your process/control maturity. Process maturity is derived from the maturity state of the individual controls within the process. The states indicated with '**Y**' indicate criteria to be fulfilled for a given process/control to increase the maturity level.

For example, a Level 5 process/control has to be recognized as required, responsibility assigned to an individual, desired state documented, actual state regularly audited for compliance and the control activities automated using tool.

The evaluation table provides a mechanism to quantify the current state and target state of IT process maturity.

### DMAIC: **Improve**

Table 4.9 shows how to get your Improve phase on track. Table 4.10 and 4.11 provide forms with suggestions on how to document these steps.

| | | Criteria - Is the process under control? | | | | |
|---|---|---|---|---|---|---|
| Level | Description | Recognized? | Assigned? | Documented? | Audited? | Automated? |
| 0 | **Non-existent -** Process doesn't exist | | | | | |
| 1 | **Initial** - Process is ad hoc and disorganized | Y | | | | |
| 2 | **Repeatable** - Process follows a regular pattern | Y | Y | | | |
| 3 | **Defined** - Processes are documented and communicated | Y | Y | Y | | |
| 4 | **Managed** - Processes are monitored and measured | Y | Y | Y | Y | |
| 5 | **Optimized** - Processes are followed and automated | Y | Y | Y | Y | Y |

Table 4.8 Process/control maturity evaluation table

## 4.4.3   Phase 3 - Sustain the Future State

Unless Phase 3 is completed, the business value for the project undertaken would not be realized. The benefits can be maximized by completing Phase 3 in the minimum time possible.

The ultimate goal of the IT process improvement project is to maximize business value, by improving the business services. This means making IT better, faster and cheaper.

From Figure 4.5 we see that we can maximize business value for the IT process improvement projects by:

• increasing the quantum of improvement *i* through breakthrough improvement solutions
• reducing the time *t* to adopt the improvement solution by getting buy-in from the stakeholders for an improvement solution

| Step | Activity number | Activity description | Input | Output |
|------|-----------------|---------------------|-------|--------|
| | 5 | List the work breakdown structure to achieve the target maturity level for each control practice. | Table 4.7 | Table 4.10 |
| | | Register the action taken against each work breakdown activity. | | |
| **Improve** | 6 | List the target and achieved maturity level against each prioritized control practice. | Table 4.10 | Table 4.11 |
| | | List the new vital X's (Target maturity level) and define the tolerance limits. Start measuring these. | | |
| | | Populate the target value and the achieved value. | | |
| | | Populate whether the KGI/KPI values achieved are satisfactory or not. | | |
| | | If the KGI/KPI values achieved are not satisfactory then go back to step 2. | | |

Table 4.9 Improving the KGIs and KPIs

| Control practices (prioritized) | Target maturity | Process owner | Work breakdown structure | Actions taken |
|--------------------------------|-----------------|---------------|--------------------------|---------------|
| <Free text> | <Numeric> | <Free text> | <Free text> | <Free text> |

Table 4.10 Form for *Improve-5* step

| Control practices (prioritized) | Target maturity | Achieved maturity | Related KGI/KPI | Target value | Achieved value | Results satisfactory? |
|---|---|---|---|---|---|---|
| <Free text> | <Numeric> | <Numeric> | <Free text> | <Numeric> | <Numeric> | <Yes/No> |

Table 4.11 Form for *Improve-6* step

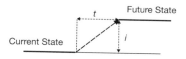

*i* - represents quantum of improvement achieved through transformation solution
*t* - represents the time taken to adopt and stabilize the transformation solution
Business value α *i* (the more the quantum of improvement, the more is the value)
Bussines value α 1/*t* (the less time is taken for change, the more is value)

Figure 4.5 Business value of an IT process improvement project

The quantum of improvement is determined in the *Recognize* phase. As seen from Figure 4.5, to maximize on the business value of the IT process improvement project we need to have a high value of *i*. This can be realized by choosing breakthrough improvement projects. Incremental improvement projects represent a lower *i*.

The *Transform* phase focuses on maximizing the quantum of improvement. To maximize the business value of the process improvement project we need to work out plans to minimize *t*.

Time *t* represents the time taken to change from current state to future state. Because *t* represents time to change, we must focus on how to handle the change transition process.

DMAIC: **Control**

It is possible to minimize *t* by adopting organizational Change Management techniques. A *control plan* should be put in place to:

- identify, analyze and correct variations with respect to the IT process improvement solution. This part of the control plan will be designed and validated in the analyze and improve phases
- handle the Change Management aspects of adopting the improvement solution. Some aspects of what should be included in the Change Management plan is described in this section

A control plan to handle organizational Change Management aspects should at the minimum include:

- **Clearly defined current state problem statement (for example Need to Change)** - the plan should clearly communicate the problem that will be solved by adopting the IT process improvement solution. The need to change should be clear and should easily connect with all the stakeholders.
- **Clearly defined future state** - the plan should clearly communicate what the IT process improvement solution is leading towards. The steady state of the improved future state should be visible to all the stakeholders.
- **Clear road map from current state to the future state** - the plan should define how the transition from current state to the future state will be achieved.
- **How to handle supporters and challengers** - the plan should identify approaches in response to those who support and challenge the IT process improvement solution.
- **How to identify and activate distributed leadership** - the plan should identify and activate distributed leadership across stakeholders. This will ensure that multiple individuals across stakeholders commit to making the improvement change happen.
- **How to generate commitment amongst stakeholders** - the plan should ensure that stakeholders are willing and able to adopt the improved IT processes.

Other proven organizational Change Management techniques should be used during the phase to minimize the time taken to adopt the improved IT processes.

## 4.5 IT process improvement – the project approach

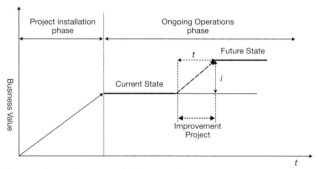

Figure 4.6 IT process improvement initiative as a project

Figure 4.6 shows that enhancing business value during the operations phase by moving from a current state to a future state is best represented as an improvement *project*.

The IT process improvement effort has the following characteristics:
- There is a well defined unique goal that initiates the IT process improvement effort.
- The process improvement goal has to be achieved within a budgeted time and cost constraint.
- The scope of the improvement effort and results has to be well defined to set expectations and focus resources.

- There are risks associated with the effort that may prevent the improvement benefits from being fully realized.
- Relevant subject matter experts come together temporarily to achieve the stated improvement goal.

All the above stated characteristics lead us to believe that IT process improvement is a *project*. Hence proven project management techniques to handle the IT process improvement effort can yield benefits in terms of:
- establishing clear and achievable goals
- balancing the competing demands or constraints for quality, scope, time and cost
- adapting the plans and approach to the different concerns and expectations of the various stakeholders
- reducing the risks and increasing the probability of successful achievement of stated goals

Once we recognize the IT process improvement effort as a *project* we can deploy the mature project management techniques to increase the probability of success on IT process improvement initiatives.

There are many project management techniques available, two of them being PRINCE2 and PMBoK:
- **PRINCE2 -** *PRojects IN Controlled Environments (PRINCE)* is a structured method for effective project management, published by OGC, UK.
- **PMBoK –** *A guide to the Project Management Body of Knowledge (PMBoK)* aims at identifying the major elements of the body of knowledge that are generally recognized as good practice. It is published by the USA Project Management Institute (PMI).

Individuals can choose their source of reference for the project management best practices depending on individual or organizational preference.

## 4.6 IT process mapping

> *A process is a set of logically linked activities that convert **inputs** provided by suppliers into desired **output** that is perceived as value by the customer receiving it.*

Process mapping is a graphic display of the activities and workflow that constitute a process. Process maps draw a picture that allow the reader to 'visualize' the process flow. 'A picture is worth a thousand words.' These process 'pictures' allow the reader to see the process inputs and outputs as well as links to other processes. By linking all the process maps together, we can verify that all the individual processes flow appropriately and that references from one map to another make sense. This makes it easier for analyzing controls and evaluating the impact of deleting, adding or modifying any activity.

An IT process document should include the following key process elements:
* goal or purpose
* scope
* roles and responsibilities
* Key Goal Indicators and Key Performance Indicators
* flowcharts depicting:
  - suppliers and inputs
  - outputs and customers
  - sub-processes, activity workflow
  - process and activity owners
  - resources
  - interactions with other IT processes.

If relevant, compliance mapping to best practices or standards should be attempted by numbering the sub-processes and activities.

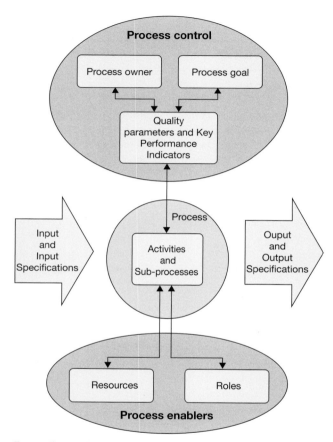

Figure 4.7 Elements of an IT process representation (source: OGC)

## 4.7 Summary

We have learned how to use the Six Sigma formula $Y = f(X_1 \, X_2 \, X_3 \, X_4 \, X_n)$ in IT process improvement, as well as how to embed the DMAIC approach in the IT process improvement phases *recognize, transform to* and *sustain the future state*.

The single most critical element of any IT process improvement project, however, is a positive mindset. The genesis of any improvement is the ability of the individual to dream and desire a future state.

Any improvement is realized twice: once in the mind of people desiring the future state and again when the believers make the future state a reality in their area of work.

# Appendix A:
# Six Sigma Glossary

Key concepts and terminologies have been selected to be meaningful for IT Service Management.

- **Continual Improvement** - A foundational element of Total Quality Management (TQM) and Deming's Plan, Do, Check, Act (PDCA) cycle. Continual Improvement stresses proactively monitoring process performance against ever-changing and evolving customer needs to continually mature the organization's ability to achieve customer-defined quality.
- **Control chart** - A statistical tool to track process performance over time. Users look out for abnormal behavior in the data points such as deviation from the centerline and/or abnormal patterns. The centerline is bound by an upper and lower limit (+/- three times the standard deviation from the mean). For example: this helps as a predictive method to catch degradation in service performance. Different types of Control charts are used depending on the type of data: variable or discrete (attribute) data.
- **Cost of Poor Quality (COPQ)** - A measure of cost based on the impact on the business caused by under performing service or process.
- **Critical to Quality (CTQ)** - Measurable characteristics and requirements that are critical to the customers and the business.
- **Defects** – A defect is a failure to meet the specified requirement, but it is also anything that inhibits, limits or compromises the delivery of a service. For example:
  - Total time a service should be available is considered an opportunity and the time that the service is unavailable during that time is a defect. Total of 43,140 minutes (opportunity for September minus 60 minutes scheduled downtime). Service outage occurred for 10 minutes

on a Monday and 1 minute on a Friday outside of the scheduled downtime. Total defect is 11 minutes (10min + 1min).

- Batch jobs, the opportunity count would be 30 for every day in September - if the batch job fails twice that month, the defect count would be two.

- **DMAIC** - An acronym for Define, Measure, Analyze, Improve and Control. DMAIC is the five phases of the Six Sigma quality improvement process. The phases are covered during a Six Sigma project using supporting techniques relevant to each phase:

  - *Define* - The key objectives in the Define phase is to scope a project in terms of the CTQ processes to be investigated and the current COPQ resulting from defects in a process. The tasks in this phase ensure that everyone involved understands the problem, the impact, and goals.

  - *Measure* - Relevant data is collected in this phase on existing process quality. Tasks include identifying the CTQ measures and evaluating the availability of measures and the accuracy, integrity, capability and dependability of the measurement system.

  - *Analyze* - Root causes of the problem are identified using the data collected in the previous phase. This enables the team to assess the impact, mitigate risks and provide the necessary information to design a solution.

  - *Improve* - During the Improve phase, action items are developed, solutions assessed and the best solution(s) recommended and implemented.

  - *Control* - The Control phase ensures the stability and predictability of the improved process, and more importantly, meeting the customers' requirements. Documenting the new processes, training appropriate staff, and continuous measurement and reporting to avoid slippage are necessary.

- **Failure Modes and Effects Analysis (FMEA)** - A process to mitigate risk by identifying potential failures and effects of the failures on a process or a service. The FMEA prioritizes potential failures through a risk rating system which uses a score of one to ten for severity, probability and detectability of failure. The potential failure with the highest Risk Priority Number (RPN) is given priority to improve. RPN is calculated by multiplying the three numbers (severity, probability, detectability). FMEA provides an important step and input into a service improvement project.

- **Key Process Input Variables (KPIV)** - One of the outputs of an initial process mapping exercise which identifies those variables, either controllable or uncontrollable, that influence the outcome of a process. In general, KPIVs are KPOVs from other, *upstream* processes.

- **Key Process Output Variables (KPOV)** - One of the outputs of an initial process mapping exercise which identifies those variables that result from a process. In general, KPOVs are KPIVs to other, *downstream* processes.

- **Mean** - An estimate of the average value in a population.

- **Minitab** - Statistical analysis software used in training as well as college and university programs.

- **Opportunity** - Any chance that a process, service or product meets requirements.

- **Pareto Principle** - Italian economist Vilfredo Pareto coined the 80/20 rule: 80% of the problems results from 20% of the sources, ie the majority of the problems are caused by the vital few issues.

- **Pareto Charts** - A graphical technique that brings focus to improve the 'vital few' causes of problems using the 80/20 rule. The Pareto Chart is a descending ordered bar chart with a cumulative percentage line. The bars indicate the number of occurrences for each cause/category of the problem and the line helps identify the vital few causes. For example, identifying the key causes in the IT infrastructure that are causing the majority of the problems. Focusing on improving those key areas that are critical to quality will have great impact on the business.

- **Plan-Do-Check-Act (PDCA)** - An underlying principle of Total Quality Management (TQM) that presents improvement as a cycle of planning what should be done (Plan), execute against those plans (Do), learn from the execution if the activity delivered what was expected

(Check), and adjust the plan to accommodate what was learned (Act). PDCA was originally introduced by Walter Shewhart and restated by Edwards Deming as the Plan-Do-Study-Act (PDSA) cycle.

- **Process** - A sequence of activities with an objective that transform inputs into outputs to deliver a service or product or to accomplish a specific task.

- **Process Map** - Any one of a variety of process charting or analysis techniques used for Six Sigma to understand how a process works, its inputs, outputs, customers, stakeholders and product or service.

- **Process Sigma Value or Sigma Quality Level** - A calculated measure of quality that determines if the performance of a process or service meets the requirements. This measure ties to the opportunity and defect counts. A six sigma measure corresponds to 3.4 defects per million opportunities. This value represents a key metric for IT service quality and allows comparisons over different processes.

- **Quality Function Deployment (QFD)** - A graphical technique that may be used early in the design of a service and then managed and modified throughout the service design and implementation project. The QFD is a planning tool that helps translate the Voice of the Customer (VOC) into the Critical to Quality (CTQs) elements and functional and non-functional requirements. Its value lies in evaluating how the organization will (or does) address what is important to the customer.

- **Run chart** - The run chart provides a means to look at trends and patterns which provide insight to potential problems, root cause and process instability manifested by variations around the median. It is particularly effective in the hands of an experienced Six Sigma Belt who will be sensitive to patterns and variation indicators of special causes of variation, such as several points sloping upward or a significant number of points above the median. These are worthy of further investigation as potential problem areas to be improved.

- **Sigma** - Describes the standard deviation, to gage the consistency of a process. Sigma is the Greek letter $\sigma$.

- **SIPOC Analysis** – Acronym for Supplier, Input, Process, Output, Customer. An improvement approach that examines a process from the perspective of the relationships between the Supplier, Input, Process, Output and Customer. The logic of this process-flow perspective provides a means to understand what goes into delivering to a customer and how those inputs may be measured.
- **Standard deviation** - An estimate of the spread around an average in a population.
- **Variables** - Those elements, characteristics or quantities that are part of a process that may change when repeated. Since, by definition, variables are subject to change, it is important to identify all variables associated with any process targeted for improvement.
- **Variance** - Mathematically defined as the average squared deviation form the mean, the variance provides a precise measure of variation.
- **Variation** - Deviation from an agreed or accepted standard or a deviation from expectations. There are two sources of variation:
  - *common (or chance) cause variation* - variation that is inherent in, naturally occurring within a system
  - *special (or assignable) cause* - variation that may be traced (or assigned) to a specific, identifiable cause or event

    Edwards Deming would say that common or chance variation is the responsibility of management to rectify. Special cause variation can be identified and then eliminated by a process improvement expert. A process that is considered to be in statistical control (and is therefore predictable) is free of special cause variation.
- **Voice of the Customer (VOC)** - Captures the Critical to Quality (CTQs) requirements of the clients or end-users in the form of surveys, interviews, complaint logs, focus groups et cetera. This is also important to capture and measure the 'perception' of- versus the 'actual' service quality from the customers perspective.

# Appendix B: Managing the Six Sigma project in practice

What actions should be taken to manage your Six Sigma improvement project well and what pitfalls should you be aware of? The tables below aim at giving an overview for each phase of the DMAIC(R) model. The time figures for implementation provide an example estimation. They will vary depending on multiple factors such as size and complexity of the organization, project and the size of the project team.

## DMAIC: Define

| Phase: | Task | Deliverables | Tools | Application | Pitfalls | Time |
|---|---|---|---|---|---|---|
| 1 | Select and approve Six Sigma Project. | Completed mandate signed off by Black Belt, champion and financial controller. | Stakeholder analysis, financial benefit analysis. | Before start of project to assess viability. | Mandate not completely filled out and signed off resulting in risks. | 1 wk |

**DMAIC: Measure**

| Phase: | Task | Deliverables | Tools | Application | Pitfalls | Time |
|--------|------|--------------|-------|-------------|----------|------|
| 1 | Define External CTQ (Critical to Quality parameter). | External CTQ defined in text in direct correlation to customer needs and financial benefit of the project. | None. The potential improvement on the external CTQ reflects the benefits of the project. | External CTQ serves as the dependent variable during the project. | External CTQ not 100% correlated with project goals. | 1 wk |
| 2 | Select and define the correct Internal CTQs in direct relation with the external CTQ. | Internal CTQ defined in text in direct correlation the external CTQ. | Correlation graph CTQ-flowdown Pareto-analysis Tree diagram = CTQ-flowdown Customer Needs Mapping (CNM). | Describe the relationship between external CTQ and internal CTQs. | Selected internal CTQs do not have a clear relation with the external CTQ. | 2 wk |
| 3 | Operationalize the external and internal CTQs. | Accurate, mutually exclusive, numerical and / or mathematical definition. | Definition fits into: Unit Defect Opportunity LSL + USL Population. | Necessary to quantify CTQs and to assign a unit of measurement to them. | CTQs not operationalized in a clear and numerical manner, unit of measurement subject to debate. | 1 wk |

| | | | | | | |
|---|---|---|---|---|---|---|
| 4 | Define procedure of measurement for the Int CTQs. | Defined measurement procedure per Int CTQ. | None. Depends on the type of CTQ and the matching unit of measurement. | Necessary to be able to measure the int CTQs. | Time consuming and / or unreliable procedure of measurement. | 1 wk |
| 5 | Validate the procedure of measurement. | Measurement report including: validity; resolution; bias; stability; linearity; reproducibility; repeatability. | Continuous data: Gauge R&R Nominal data: Kappa-analysis Ordinal data: Kappa & ICC. | For reliable findings, valid measurements are the absolute cornerstone! | Data from systems that are accurate, but do not reflect to the definition of what should have been measured. | 2 wk |
| 6 | Perform measurement according to the approved measurement procedure. Int CTQ is measured. | Sufficient reliable and representative data on Int CTQs (= process) available. | In case of sample, the sample methods: single a-select; a-select; systematic; stratified. When population available, use all data. | Int CTQs are being measured so the process capability can be assessed. | Wrong method of sampling, insufficient data; uncontrolled measurements. | 6 wk |

DMAIC: **Analyze**

| Phase: | Task | Deliverables | Tools | Application | Pitfalls | Time |
|---|---|---|---|---|---|---|
| 1 | Assess the process capability (How does the internal CTQ perform against USL and LSL?). | Process USL and LSL are mapped, process has been measured according to procedure. Control chart and PCA ready. | Control charts; Process-capability analysis (PCA) (Cp & Cpk; Z-values; waste%) Box-plot; Normal Distribution. | Provides insight into process behaviour, distribution of data and disruptions. | Mixing up of UCL and LCL with USL and LSL. Control limits are *not* specification limits! | 1 wk |
| 2 | Define final project goal. | Described diagnosis of process capability, final savings; goal-average, spread (short and long term) versus INT CTQ. | Benchmarking; Process Capability Analysis, Project Mandate for calculation of final projected savings. | Provides a realistic goal in terms of financial benefits of the project. | Method of calculation of provisional savings of mandate not adhered to for calculation final predicted savings. | 1 wk |
| 3 | Determine potential influence factors that influence the Int CTQ(s). | Pinpoint as many possible influence factors per process step as possible that may have an impact on the Int CTQ. | Control charts, Exploratory Data Analysis, Fishbone Diagram, FMEA, Brainstorm session, Process Matrix. | Provides an overview of potential influence factors on Int CTQ (the X-s). | Assessing the Int CTQ as an influence factor on the Ext CTQ. Do not do this, there should be a relationship as in *Measure* step 2. | 3 wk |

# DMAIC: Improve

| Phase: | Task | Deliverables | Tools | Application | Pitfalls | Time |
|---|---|---|---|---|---|---|
| 1 | Measure the potential influence factors (Xs) in relation to the Int CTQs. | Set of data (sample, population, experiments) that connects Xs with Int CTQs for hypothesis testing. | Sampling, collecting available data. Should data not be available; Design of Experiments (DoE). | Generates data on Xs that can subsequently be tested for influence on the Int CTQ. | Incorrect definition of Experiment, wrong sample techniques, historical data which is still unreliable. | 3 wk |
| 2 | Test the data in order to separate the vital few influence factors that really affect Int CTQs from the trivial many with insignificant impact. | List of vital influence factors on Int CTQ as well as the mathematical equation which describe this influence (Transfer function). | Data-analysis through: Regression DoE / GLM ANOVA Kruskal-Wallis Logistic Regression Chi-square. | Provide a transfer function of vital Xs in relation to the Int CTQ. The Int CTQ can now be predicted from various X-values. | Selection of false hypothesis test in order to establish vital Xs and their connection the Int CTQ. False interpretation of p-values from testing. | 1 wk |

| Phase | Task | Deliverables | Tools | Application | Pitfalls | Time |
|---|---|---|---|---|---|---|
| 3 | Design improvements to keep all vital Xs into their optimal settings in order to optimize the Int CTQ. | Accurately described improvements on vital Xs to allow these to set the Int CTQ to optimal value and have the Ext CTQ perform at its best. | Optimization of each X in transfer function through graphical method or classical function analysis, yielding the measures to be taken. | Describes for each vital X its optimal mean and max allowed variation in order to yield an optimal Int CTQ value. | Incorrect interpretation of transfer function where Xs predict the outcome in Int CTQ leading to suboptimial or even adverse Int CTQ-values. | 2 wk |
| 4 | Produce a business case and present the findings of the project to Black Belt, champion and financial controller. Their sign-off closes the investigation. | Completed business case with the improvement measures, statistical proof, and final savings prediction as well as cost of implementation. | Net present value method, Risk analysis, project plan. | Describes the measures needed to attain statistical success resulting in optimal mean and variance. | Vague description of measures, their cost and their impact on mean and spread in Int CTQ making handover for implementation tricky and risky. | 1 wk |
| <<Implementation through project management method>> | | | | | | |
| | Implement the improvements as agreed upon in the business case | Implemented improvements, optimized process, signed off by steering | Selected Project Management method. | Ensures proper application of improvements. | Insufficient communication between Green Belt and project | According to project plan. |

## DMAIC: Control

| Phase: | Task | Deliverables | Tools | Application | Pitfalls | Time |
|--------|------|--------------|-------|-------------|----------|------|
| 1 | Embed the improvements into the quality assurance system and into each process. | Continuous Process measurements have been set up, procedures have been adjusted. | Process Owner; process Dashboard; OCAP; Poka Yoke; control plan and control loops; Mistake Proofing. | Provides feedback on vital Xs, their impact on Int CTQ and methods of control. | Quality Assurance and management not involved. No follow-up from the Green Belt. | 3 wk |
| 2 | Establish new process capability. | Process capability of altered process, final savings calculated and signed off by financial controller. | Control charts on Xs and Int CTQ, Periodical Process Capability Analysis. | Calculates improvement in process and proves final savings. | No continuous measurement of Xs and Int CTQ, of just measuring outcomes (Int CTQ). | 4 to 20 wk |
| 3 | Close the project | Hand over the project to management. Continue to provide statistical assistance. | None. | None. | No permanent support arranged. | 1 wk |

DMAIC: **Report (Optional but important phase)**

| Phase: | Task | Deliverables | Tools | Application | Pitfalls | Time |
|--------|------|--------------|-------|-------------|----------|------|
| 1 | Design a new reporting method. | Standard method of periodical reporting. | Control chart, capability analysis. | Share success, ensure lasting improvements. | No financial benefits calculated or project success not shared. | Up to one year. |

# Appendix C: Techniques that can be used in ITSM Six Sigma projects

This section provides a partial list of Six Sigma techniques based on the case studies from the *Six Sigma for IT Management* book.

These definitions include graphical representation, phase of the DMAIC and ITIL process(es) that they support. Some of the following techniques may be best suited for advanced Six Sigma practitioners; however, with more service management products automating Six Sigma techniques for IT data makes it much easier to apply and understand.

It is important to note that any improvement campaign should be carefully managed by an experienced project manager within a project framework that evaluates feasibility, clarity of goals, budget and scope. The project should also provide clear communications, identify the key stakeholders and responsibilities, and design a pilot that validates the direction.

## C.1 Cause and Effect (Fishbone or Ishikawa) diagram

This helps to get a clear understanding of the causes and effects of the problem in the Define phase. It is used to find all the factors that influence an outcome. Potential problem areas are being mapped onto this diagram, for example, during a brainstorming session. These results can be used as input for the Failure Mode and Effects Analysis (FMEA).

The C&E Diagram helps focus on the causes of the issues that need to be solved. Inputs include:
• the CTQs from the early Voice of the Customer surveys

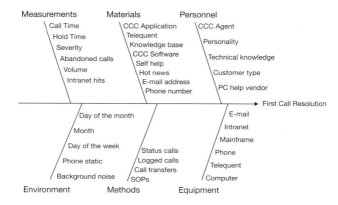

Figure C.1 Cause and Effect Diagram Service Desk

- the CTQ components in the CTQ Tree
- the controllable and non-controllable KPIVs from the process map
- the metrics from the process assessments

It provides a visual representation of the relevant variables impacting the failure to deliver consistent service and can be used to brainstorm and explore possible causes of an issue, across several dimensions:

- **wide perspective** - as a brainstorming exercise, it provides a framework enabling all parties to offer their view
- **categorize** – it helps categorize the possible causes by providing the framework within which causes can be organized. This benefit is often overlooked
- **focus** - it focuses on the critical issues that require further investigation

## C.2 Cause and Effects (C&E) Matrix

The list of potential causes of the problem can grow exponentially. While the C&E diagram is an essential first step, the scope should be narrowed.

First, 'Where to focus? If focus is narrowed too drastically, a critical variable could be overlooked.

The C&E Matrix provides a way to correlate potential causes with the customer requirements as captured by the CTQs. It provides the disciplined structure necessary to weigh and correlate the possible causes, providing a level of focus that is not possible in the C&E Diagram alone.

The C&E Matrix can be constructed out of the process steps and the outputs documented in the process map. The high-level customer CTQs are listed across the header of the table and assigned a numerical rating for importance to the customer.

Customer representatives can be engaged to aid in defining the importance of each CTQ element. Each customer CTQ can be rank-ordered on a 1 to 10 scale where '1' means least important and '10' is deemed most important. The inputs can be listed along the stub and assigned a weight as to the degree to which they influence the CTQ. Weighting criteria can assign a numerical weight to each input. For example, four levels, 0, 1, 3, and 9 can be assigned a correlation score:

0 = no correlation

1 = minimal correlation

3 = moderate correlation

9 = strong correlation.

A '9' can be selected for 'strong correlation' to force discrimination in the weighting criteria. Cross multiplying the CTQ 'level of importance' rating and the input correlation score, those inputs with the greatest correlation with (having the greatest impact on) the CTQs can be easily identified.

If the exercise yields a rather large number of what appears to be very important inputs, some of the correlations may have been overstated:

- if all inputs are determined to have high correlation, the project might become unwieldy and difficult to manage. A more focused strategy is then required
- relying exclusively on a rigid mathematical prioritization process may have overshadowed the experienced insight of team members

To ensure insight is not sacrificed for rigid adherance to a process, the C&E Matrix may be revisited several times. Customers should again be involved to re-validate the CTQs 'level of importance priority factor'. As each subsequent matrix is completed, the number of inputs should be sequentially pruned, effectively narrowing the focus to a manageable number.

# C.3 Communication plan

With the charter in place the project stakeholder matrix can be used to build an integrated communication plan. Although the charter is designed to gain support for the project, the changes that will ultimately arise from the intervention will likely meet some level of resistance. This plan should be designed to deal with the potential resistance by:

- reaching out to the key stakeholders
- providing project status reports
- explaining and reiterating the 'what's in it for me' value of the project
- getting feedback which would be used to proactively address potential new barriers to success
- leveraging the existing communications infrastructure where possible
- developing new means of communications if necessary
- driving and reinforcing accountability as set forth in the charter
- maintaining momentum for the project

Nothing should be left to chance. The communication plan should focus on delivering specific content to the relevant stakeholders using the most appropriate medium. Each communication has a topic owner, clearly documented objectives, and, more importantly, specifies what the recipient is expected to do with the information. As with any effective plan, metrics are to be developed to monitor execution.

## C.4 Control chart

Control charts help identify issues in service level performance if, for example, the response time trendline deviates from the mean. Some organizations have tied the control limits with automated alert notifications to ensure issues are spotted before they affect the business.

Control charts highlight any abnormal behaviour and also offer a safeguard in case any important metrics are missed. If the trendline goes 'out of control' for no apparent reason then the IT department should investigate to see if an IT system might be contributing to the issue, or a non IT event such as a sale by a competitor. This information should also be available to the business users to assist with their decision-making processes.

For example, when measuring an application's performance, an e-credit card payment application response time may vary from the mean during lunch hours and on Fridays (Figure C.2). This might then be further investigated.

The control chart proves valuable in both the Measure and Analyze phases, and should be maintained as well over the Control phase to keep track of the process' performance. This allows the IT department to show how improvement to IT systems through Six Sigma has a direct impact on the profitability of the business and provides IT a means to proactively monitor abnormal trends that could potentially be caused by IT issues.

| Communication | Audience | Methods | Frequency | Reason | Response |
|---|---|---|---|---|---|
| Project Charter – Executive Summary Presentations | Executive Sponsor(s) PMO Management Program Managers Security team Account Services Finance, budgeting HR | **Active:** Formal Meetings **Passive:** -Distributed documents -Distributed Intranet link | End of planning and analysis – currently on-going | Review scope and project organization | Approval of scope and project organization |
| Program Kick-off | All impacted parties | **Active:** Formal, mandatory meeting | One time only *(multiple as necessary to accommodate schedules)* | Set expectations | Support and comprehension of objectives |
| Status Report | Customers, Key Stakeholders | **Passive:** Distributed Intranet link via 'Monthly Broadcast' | Monthly | - Reinforce program objectives - Build stakeholder communication - Communicate current involvements, accomplishments | Questions, related initiatives, new initiatives |
| | Management | **Active:** Regular agenda item in standing Management meeting | Weekly | - Communicate accomplishments, changes -Direction, guidance, advice | Continued support and understanding of program |
| | | **Passive:** Performance Reporting via 'Monthly Broadcast' | Monthly | Appendix D | |
| | | **Passive:** Email | Weekly | | |

Table C.1 A communication plan outlining 'who', 'what', 'where', 'when', and 'why' of communications.

Payments - eCreditCard

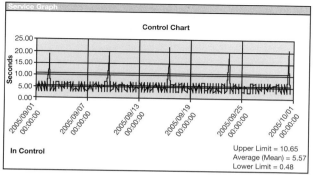

Figure C.2 Control chart payments eCreditCard: poor response times on Fridays

## C.5 Control plan

The control plan seeks to ensure that the improvements become institutionalized and that the process will not revert to its previous, unimproved state. It includes all that a process owner needs to understand about how the process has been improved, the process and sub-process maps, all input and output variables, training, documentation and recommended action if the process begins to drift out of control. It also establishes measures to keep track of the process.

To this aim, the high level cross-functional process flow chart developed as part of the training improvement initiative is expanded to include the interfaces, inputs and outputs, between the three functional groups. In addition to the process flow the plan includes:

- measures and monitoring requirements and Key Performance Indicators (KPIs) that are regularly reported to monitor the health of the process
- threshold measures at the critical thresholds between each process interface point. A run chart with control limits provided a continuing health-check on the process and a reference for the process owner

- at each of these monitored interface points a plan of action (a response plan) details the action should the data appear to be trending out of control. This leaves no doubt to the required response to maintain the process
- the plan includes a regular audit of all the performance measures. This is reported, regularly reviewed and acted upon

Like any form of documentation, it is a 'controlled document', which means it is subject to documentation versioning standards, resides in a restricted repository, is subject to change control and is regularly reviewed and updated as necessary.

| Process | Process Step | Output | Input | Specifications (Limit or Target) | Control Method | Sampling Frequency | Action Plan |
|---------|--------------|--------|-------|----------------------------------|----------------|--------------------|-------------|
| Change | Create Change Record | Change Record | RFC | 100% Changes Use RFC | Audit | Weekly | Training |
| | Assign Change Priority | Prioritized Change | Change Record | 100% Changes Assigned Priority | Audit | Weekly | SOP |

Table C.2 Management control plan

## C.5.1 Control plan calendar

The control plan is a living document and, as already stated, subject to change as conditions (or planned revisions and reviews) dictate. The control plan calendar expands on the fields above to add detail and accountability for ongoing process control and reporting.

| Task | Description | Responsible | Aug | Sep | Oct | Nov | Dec |
|------|-------------|-------------|-----|-----|-----|-----|-----|
| RFC Audit/Report | Changes Using RFCs | Change Mgr. | X | X | X | X | X |
| Priority Audit | Priority accurately assigned | Change Admin | X | X | X | X | X |

Table C.3 Control plan calendar

## C.6 CTQ - Critical to Quality Tree

An assessment may be used to evaluate process capability (See section C.17) the output of which may be used as inputs to a CTQ Tree (see Figure C.3). Each of the customer requirements, captured as CTQs in the Define phase, can be placed on the left side of a simple tree structure. Each CTQ requirement is then evaluated as to the components that comprised the requirement. This 'decomposition' provides an enhanced definition of the CTQ. Each component is then decomposed again into the data elements that might be used to measure each component.

Inputs to this step include:
- CTQ Requirements from the Define phase
- Key Process Input Variables (KPIVs) and Key Process Output Variables (KPOVs) from the detailed process mapping exercise
- metrics from the process assessment (see section C16)

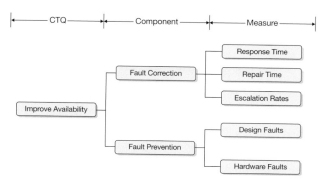

Figure C.3 Simplified CTQ Tree to decompose customer requirements

Once the CTQ Tree is fully decomposed working from the high level CTQs on the left toward the metrics components on the right, it becomes clear which metrics are available and where potential measurement gaps exist.

Once these measures are identified, baseline data that are to be monitored throughout the project can be gathered. Measures needed for proceeding with the project can be established as well.

## C.7 Design of Experiments

Design of Experiments (DoEs) are used to determine significant factors that affect output or results and can be performed to determine how significant a solution thought of in the Analyze phase might actually be.

**Response was "First Contact Resolution" Yes/No**
**Fractional Factorial Fit: FCR y/n versus knowledge, remote**
*Estimated effects and coefficients for FCR y/n (coded units)*

| Term | Effect | Coef | SE Coef | T | P | |
|------|--------|------|---------|---|---|---|
| Constant | | 1.4583 | 0.07553 | 19.31 | 0.000 | |
| Knowledge | 0.4167 | 0.2083 | 0.07553 | 2.76 | 0.012 | |
| Remote | 0.5833 | 0.2917 | 0.07553 | 3.86 | 0.001 | |
| | | | | | | |

*Analysis of variance for FCR y/n (coded units)*

| Source | DF | Seq SS | Adj SS | Adj MS | F | P |
|--------|----|--------|--------|--------|---|---|
| Main effects | 2 | 3.08333 | 3.08333 | 1.54167 | 11.26 | 0.000 |
| Residual error | 21 | 2.87500 | 2.87500 | 0.13690 | | |
| Lack of fit | 1 | 0.04167 | 0.04167 | 0.04167 | 0.29 | 0.594 |
| Pure error | 20 | 2.83333 | 2.83333 | 00.4167 | | |
| Total | 23 | 5.95833 | | | | |

Table C.4 DoE indicates the significance of different tools to FCR

For example, if the use of a knowledge base tool and a Remote Administration tool would actually increase a Service Desk's First Contact Resolution (FCR, see Table C.4).

The results indicate that Remote Control has a greater effect on FCR than a knowledge base tool, but both are significant as indicated by *Six Sigma P-value*.

The P-value indicates which variable has a greater effect on the results. A low P-value indicates a high correlation. Both Main Effects (knowledge base and remote administration) are significant. The high P-value for the lack of fit indicates a 'good fit' model.

# C.8 Failure Mode and Effects Analysis (FMEA)

Failure Modes and Effects Analysis (FMEA) helps assess the risks and impact of IT components and services on the business. Although FMEA is similar to ITIL's Component Failure Impact Analysis (CFIA), CFIA lacks FMEA's Risk Priority Number (RPN) concept for prioritization (including ranking severity, probability and detectability of failures).

The FMEA further defines The Xs and Ys from the process map and Cause and Effect Diagram (Table C.5). Once the inputs and outputs of each process step are determined, the FMEA is used to prioritize issues and begin brainstorming on possible solutions. Each X and Y is identified and prioritized based on severity, occurrence, and level of detection. This way, the 'Key Processes' impacting the desired outcome (Y=f(X)) can be found.

## C.8.1 FMEA Steps:

Four basic steps are necessary to complete this technique. These steps should be repeated for each Failure Mode (or potential problems), as illustrated in Table C.5:

1. Step 1 entails listing the potential Failure Modes of the service investigated. After listing the potential Failure Modes, Effects of the Failure, the Causes of the Failure and the Current Control systems to prevent the failure are identified.

2. Each identified Failure Mode is then rated for Severity, Probability, and Detectability using a score of 1-10 (10 being the highest).

| Services | Failure Mode | Effects of Failure | Severity | Causes of failure | Probability | Current Controls | Detectability | RPN |
|----------|--------------|--------------------|----------|-------------------|-------------|------------------|---------------|-----|
| Payments - e CreditCard | Payment System. Software Crashes. | Customers cannot make Credit Card Payments. | 7 | Insufficient system resources. | 3 | Only infra-structure monitoring is in place. Unable to determine if the service is available. | 7 | 147 |
| CICS - Login | CICS Region unable to process new requests. | System busy and not responding in expected time. | 6 | Insufficient resources. | 4 | No simulated login to mainframe, only infrastructure monitoring is in place. | 5 | 120 |
| Load Balancer | Load Balancer not distributing Load correctly. | Users experience slowdown as some resources are over utilized while others remain idle. | 5 | Misconfiguration of the Load Balancing Device. | 3 | No monitoring of Load Distribution. | 5 | 75 |
| Login - eCreditCard | Login System cannot verify user account with Mainframe Back End. | Users cannot log into the eCredit Card Syrem. | 5 | Mainframe is busy or network outage. | 3 | Poor ability to simulate logins to the mainframe. | 4 | 60 |
| Balance - eCreditCard | Balance not available. | Unable to retrieve account balances from mainframe. | 3 | Mainframe busy or unavailable. | 2 | No regular check of account balance functionality, although system monitoring is present. | 4 | 24 |

3. An RPN for each Failure Mode can be calculated by multiplying each score:

> **RPN Calculation:**
> **Severity X Probability X Detectability = RPN**
> 7 X 3 X 7 = 147

4. Then action items for improving each Failure Mode can be recommended. The RPNs are the mechanism to prioritize problem resolution which will mitigate risk according to business criticality. This also assures the Problem Management resources are spent on the problems that are most critical to the business.

# C.9 Gage R&R

Gage R&R measures repeatability, reliability and reproducibility, in other words: process consistency.

It can, for example, be conducted to ensure Service Desk agents interpret and document customer requests consistently.

This tool looks at the variation in measurement data employing one measuring instrument and several operators. To demonstrate this, each agent can be asked to report on ten specific customer requests.

The Gage R&R in Figure C.4 shows that there is no consistency in how various requests are handled. The variation is with 'repeatability'. There is no consistency in an agent's response to the same type of request.

To find out what causes this inconsistency, standard operating procedures should be reviewed. An obvious process to evaluate would be the filling out of call tickets. Possible causes that may be found:
• Service Desk agents interpret customer requests differently due to lack of training and experience. For example, an experienced Agent would

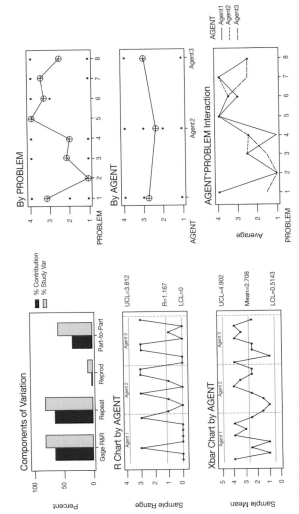

Figure C.4 Gage R&R of agents and requests

respond to a request as 'logged' because he/she knew the answer through experience, while a new agent would respond to a request as 'PC technician' because of their lack of experience. To improve consistency, a robust process would need to be established that would be robust and match the agent's level of experience. Current training programs as well as the tools used to maintain and share information (incidents and solutions) should be reviewed.

- The process for filling out Service Center tickets may provide too many options for the agents. When an agent needs to fill in a 'failing component', a 'resolve code', and a 'category' field from a list of more than hundred options for each field, these options will be interpreted differently by every agent and therefore lead to inconsistency.

# C.10 Gap analysis

This tool may be the precedent to additional analysis using more traditional Six Sigma tools. A properly executed gap analysis will call for deeper, more detailed analysis such as that enabled by a Pareto, run chart and statistical capability analysis.

A gap analysis might suggest some vulnerability at a specific sub-process step, say for example, the 'Update Configuration Repository' sub-process in Change Management. Additional data would be required to validate that finding. We will describe how the gap analysis might be used and then discuss Six Sigma tools that would augment the findings in a gap analysis.

The gap analysis examines one ITSM process at a time to understand at the process and even deeper, more detailed sub-process level, the gap between the current baseline and the highest level best practice.

There are a number of gap analysis methodologies, but we have found the best approach is executed following an overall process assessment (see C.16). However an assessment is inadequate in describing precisely where the process falls short. It provides an overview while the gap analysis drills deeper to understand why the process does not measure up.

However, if the goal is to target only those processes that must be improved to accommodate a specific application or service (as in the case of a Service Oriented Architecture, for example), process mapping (see C.18 and section 4.6) and use case analysis (see C.29) may be enough to identify those processes that should be subjected to the rigor of a gap analysis.

Since a gap analysis embraces the high-level process and sub-process elements specific to a given process and its necessary interface points to other IT Service Management processes, it is very effective in examining the upstream (input) and downstream (output) aspects of each process.

Although the analysis exercise compares the current state with a fully mature best practice, the highest level of maturity or capability (a Level 5, for example) is not generally the objective. An astute user of the gap analysis will think in practical terms to analyze the minimum levels of capability of the key processes supporting the customer requirements as set forth in the use cases. Such a leader will leverage the findings of a gap analysis to set the target capability level for the organization. This approach demands a thorough understanding of the requirements and is precisely why it is so important to accurately define and then analyze customer requirements.

# C.11 Histogram

The histogram is a tool to understand the centrality, spread, and shape of the data generated by the system. The histogram is particularly effective in understanding performance against customer specifications. This is apparent in the pattern of variation produced by the system.

Initial analysis will consider the various shapes common to histogram data (normal, skewed, bi-modal, random, etc) which will provide guidance as to additional stratification or cause analysis.

For example, multiple peaks in the histogram indicate that there are other factors or systems influencing the data that would require further decomposition of the data classifications (classes).

The histogram should be run before improvement and again following the intervention to evaluate the impact of the improvement effort.

## C.12 Operational definition

A fundamental principle in measurement is precision and repeatability. It helps develop clear definitions for the measures, documentation as to how the measures will be collected and, if necessary, to train the data collectors. An operational definition brings a level of structure and control to measure identification, selection and recording.

Such a definition describes the 'what', the thing, feature or defect you are trying to measure. The tool and/or the means of measurement are described in detail. Any variables relating to the measurement instrument should be specified so as to remove any doubt about the configuration of the testing instrument. How you will take the measure, the specific procedural method, clearly describes how the observation will be made and the parameters of the observation (when, where, and under which conditions).

## C.13 Pareto chart

A gap analysis (see C.10) might prompt further investigation of input or output measures. Plotting the data collected by category may highlight one or two categories of problem areas that are undermining your process. The improve efforts might then be directed at those specific areas.

By using the 80/20 rule, the Pareto chart (Figure C.5) provides a means to focus on those vital issues that offer the greatest opportunity for improvement. This way, it helps identify immediately the vital few issues that account for the majority of the problem.

This helps IT service and support staff focus on the high impact areas of Service Level Management. It highlights the root causes of poor quality, where they are not visible through the systems management tools. You should check if the outcome correlates well with, for example, the FMEA's top RPNs to validate that the improvement effort is being spent on the right areas.

The Pareto chart may also be used as a means to further categorize related causes which may be candidates to be addressed in an improvement initiative. It is particularly powerful as a communications tool to gain support for an improvement project charter.

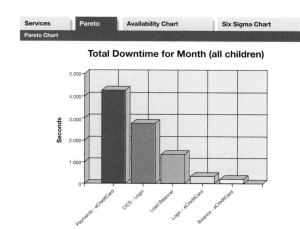

Figure C.5 Pareto chart: Highlighting the most significant issues

# C.14 Priorities or Quality Function Deployment (QFD) Matrix

The QFD Matrix helps keep all parties focused upon delivering to customer specifications. It helps define how the internal processes support the business, functional, non-functional and technical requirements.

It typically starts out as a simple priorities grid mapping customer needs against the internal processes or product features that will constitute the solution. It may be used iteratively with the customer to validate the weightings assumptions and the final prioritization.

A basic QFD Matrix might list the CTQs from the Voice of the Customer workshop across the stub. The relevant process features may then be detailed across the banner. An appropriately discriminating numerical score such as 0-1-3-9 or visual indicators using symbols can be assigned to indicate the degree of correlation between the stratified requirements and the business requirements.

This encourages discussion and further clarification of how the solution will be realized in the infrastructure. It is also an excellent tool to maintain discussions with customers and to help keep focused on the objectives of the improvement efforts.

The sample QFD matrix in Figure C.6 may be used to focus on quality as defined by the customer and is of particular value to the program manager for budgeting and planning. In this example matrix, product or process specifications that support the CTQs are featured across the matrix header. If aligned with the relevant processes, any stakeholder can see, at a glance, which processes need to be included in the improvement effort. The program manager may then use this matrix to ensure the ITIL best practices process disciplines are given due attention in planning.

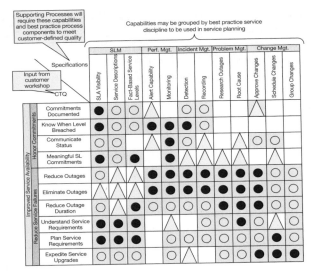

Figure C.6 Example of a Quality Function Deployment grid (A circle with a dot represents a very strong relationship. A circle indicates a strong relationship. A triangle indicates a weak relationship. No symbol represents no relationship.)

## C.15 Prioritization matrix

Table C.6 shows the result of risk analysis of only one threat. The responsible team will view the severity of all threats, the probability, and the potential loss of each threat. This enables them to find out which threats cause the greatest risk. These should be addressed first.

The team members also indicate how effective they think different control measures will be. In this case, they rate (on a scale of 1 (low) to 5 (high) a firewall, an Intrusion Detection System (IDS), and a Honeypot, a computer that has deliberate vulnerabilities, in order to entice hackers into revealing themselves.

| Threat description: hacker accessing confidential information on company file server | | | | | | |
|---|---|---|---|---|---|---|
| Team member | Threat severity | Probability | Impact | Rate the effectiveness of following controls | | |
| | | | | Firewall | Intrusion Detection System | Honeypot |
| Member 1 | 4 | 2 | 4 | 4 | 3 | 2 |
| Member 2 | 4 | 4 | 4 | 3 | 4 | 1 |
| Member 3 | 2 | 3 | 3 | 4 | 2 | 1 |
| Member 4 | 3 | 4 | 3 | 4 | 2 | 1 |
| Member 5 | 5 | 4 | 4 | 4 | 4 | 2 |
| Results | 3.6 | 3.4 | 3.6 | 3.8 | 3 | 1.4 |

Table C.6 Control selection through Prioritization matrix

## C.16 Process assessment

An assessment can be used to understand the current state of the processes underlying operations. If time constraints prohibit an exhaustive assessment of all the processes, the detailed process map can be used to identify those essential operational processes that should be assessed to understand 'infrastructure readiness' for the development activities that should soon follow. There are two criteria for selecting the processes:
• the process outputs are KPIVs to other processes
• the process has significant dependence upon the output of related processes

Figure C.7 shows a limited operations process assessment illustrating the relative maturity levels. 'Benchmark' is the best practice maturity level '5' included here for scale.

The assessment not only provides a maturity level for each infrastructure process, but identifies the process owner and the metrics used to manage the process as well as the measures and reports used to monitor the process.

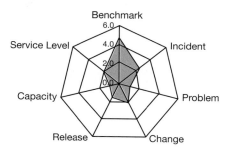

Figure C.7 Limited process assessment showing relative maturity levels

## C.17 Process capability

Process capability is the capability of the *internal CTQ* process.

> *At the Service Desk, we might look at the First Call Resolution (FCR). This can be measured through a software application managing call tickets. These tickets can be used to track the status of a request until it is resolved (closed). When a customer request can be resolved by a Customer Care Center (CCC) agent and logged in the application as a 'closed' ticket while the customer is on the phone this is defined as 'First Call Resolution' or 'FCR'. This is calculated as a percentage by taking the total number of closed tickets divided by the total number of tickets (calls) \* 100. This is then the process capability percentage we are looking for and we can derive a Sigma Value from this as well. If FCR rate is 58% or the Process Capability is 58%, the Sigma Value for this process is .22.*

Process capability should be measured at the start of a project, but also tracked over the control phase.

One way of measuring process control is Statistical Process Charting (SPC). The proportion of defects produced (number of unresolved tickets) to total number of calls taken should be measured monthly and compared to the baseline via a Binomial Capability chart. P-charts are used to measure proportional data and predetermined specification limits.

| June, 2000 | August, 2000 |
|---|---|
| CP = Zst/3 | CP = Zst/3 |
| | |
| Zlt = .23 | Zlt = .30 (long term sigma value) |
| Zst = 1.5 + .23 = 1.73 | Zst = 1.5 + .30 = 1.80 (short term sigma value) |
| Cp = 1.73/3 = 58% | CP = 1.80/3 = 60% (process capability) |

Table C.7 Process capability chart

The process capability chart (Table C.7) shows a 2% improvement in FCR in August compared to June data. The two-month improvement is an indication that progress is going in the right direction. Over time, as the Service Desk matures, these improvements will accelerate and can go up significantly.

## C.18 Process map

Process mapping helps you to understand the people, processes, technology and their relationships, thus understanding how the IT service supports the process and what infrastructure is used by the IT service. This also provides the means to collect data on how the process works and to identify data that is not currently available but needs to be located.

It also helps you to understand where the hand-offs are for the various ITIL processes. The process-map can also be used to map the Critical to Quality business processes and their underlying IT services and components. This information can then be used to create service models for business service management and Service Level Management products or vice versa.

It adds value by broadening the perspective by which one may evaluate the appropriate metrics. If used in conjunction with the use case (see C.29), the process map is an incredibly powerful instrument to specify the appropriate measures. The processs map has been explained in section 4.6, IT Process Mapping.

A process map 'walks through' the overall process from the customer's perspective. Figure C.8 shows one for the Service Desk process. Each step in the process consists of factors (Xs) that are used as 'input' to the process step. Relative to each input factor, there can be one to many different outcomes (Ys). Some of the output factors are productive while others are not.

For example, a customer has a 'request' which is a factor (X) in the first process step. The possible outcomes (Ys) are that the customer contacts the Customer Care Center (CCC), Technician Services, or finds another source to turn to. The fact that there are several possible 'outcomes', makes this process step a key input factor in the analysis.

A process map also provides insight into the make up of each of the CTQ business processes. This can later become input when creating the Service Model for the Service Level Management tool to be implemented during the improve phase. Figure C.9 shows an example of the Service Model highlighting some of the key business services based on process map information.

A detailed process map should define the Key Process Input Variables (KPIV) and Key Process Output Variables (KPOV) of the process to be improved. This may very well take several iterations, each with increasing levels of detail and complexity. Each rendition of the map should classify

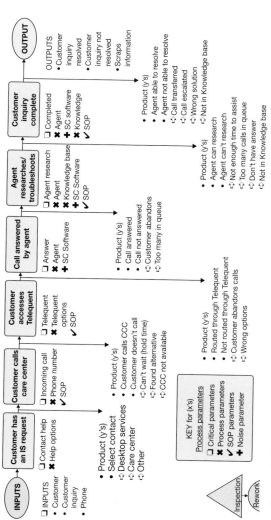

Figure C.8 Service Desk process map

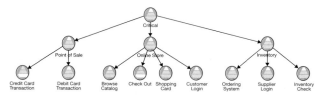

Figure C.9 Service model with key business services based on process map information

each KPIV as 'controllable', 'uncontrollable' or as a Standard Operating
Procedure (SOP):

- **controllable Input Variables** - those inputs that may be changed or
  adjusted to impact the output
- **uncontrollable Input Variables** - those inputs that are not controllable
  at all or not easily or normally controllable
- **SOP** - Standard Operating Procedure

Figure C.10 shows a simple process flow that illustrates a number of very
critical issues.

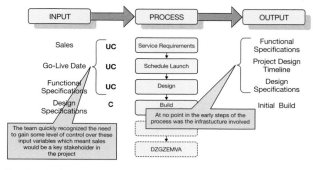

Figure C.10 Simple process flow highlighting several critical issues

This discipline helps focus on those variables that should be controlled and delivers essential data for establishing a measurement system.

## C.19 Process Sigma Value (Sigma Quality Level)

The Process Sigma Value reports the quality level of a product or service tied to the defect/opportunity count, which defects ties to costs. Using a Service Level Management example, the sigma value shows service level quality.

Take a real-world example, a bank's customers often can not make credit card payments over the Internet, the e-credit card response time data can be collected from synthetic transactions to find the corresponding sigma value. The Specification Limits taken directly from the SLA defined show that the tolerable variation in response time is between a Lower Specification Limit (LSL) of 0.48 seconds and Upper Specification Limit (USL) of 10.65 seconds (Figure C.11). The Defect defined is any transaction time exceeding the USL of 10.65 seconds, and an Opportunity the total number of e-credit card transactions occurred.

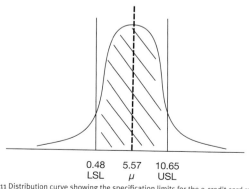

Figure C.11 Distribution curve showing the specification limits for the e-credit card response time (in seconds)

Based on these response time data collected, the sigma value is calculated to be 2.5 sigma. This represents inconsistency in e-credit card response time. The end-goal may then be to reach a level where adverse COPQ will not occur.

The process sigma value allows IT as well to compare the performance at the starting point with the improved results. Using the conversion table (Table C.8) to illustrate the defect level at the bank, this means that at 2.5 sigma, 159,000 ppm transactions fail to meet specifications. At 4.23 sigma, only 3,467 ppm transactions fail. This is a 97.8% decrease in defective transactions.

|  | Sigma Level | Defective PPM: with 1.5 sigma shift |
|---|---|---|
| Original process sigma value | 2.5 | 159,000 |
| New process sigma value | 4.23 | 3,467 |

Table C.8 Improvement results

One important aspect of the process sigma value is its non-linear relationship to defect rates. For example, a two to three sigma improvement achieves a lot more than a five to six sigma in terms of number of defects reduced. A unit shift in quality level does not correspond to a unit change in improvement. Therefore, for the bank to achieve six sigma level from 4.23 will only become more challenging.

This does not mean that the bank should start a new project immediately targeting a six sigma level. One advantage of Six Sigma is that the bank can adapt the sigma level according to clients' changing needs. As customer requirements change over time, the acceptable range of variation changes. Therefore, new specification limits and improvement initiatives are set, of course with a cost/benefit analysis and the 'cost of status-quo' in mind. To illustrate, the bank's new response time range is between 0.04 seconds and 7.58 seconds; however this may not be tolerable the next year if customers demand more or if it causes more problems. The ongoing Control phase is generally a good place for identifying issues and new improvement opportunities. This case study is further discussed in the *Six Sigma for IT Management* book.

## C.20 Project Stakeholder Matrix

If the issues to be addressed cross functional lines and are loaded with political complications and financial concerns, the SIPOC (see section C.24) can be used to prepare a 'stakeholder matrix'.

This consists of a list of the stakeholders, those with interest in the outcome of the initiative, mapped against their primary objectives (VOC and CTQ issues) and how they, either directly or indirectly, might influence the project. The matrix can be used to prepare the project charter and project communication plan. Table C.9 shows a simplified Project Stakeholder Matrix. Most improvement programs would include a more extensive list of stakeholders and their respective issues.

| Organizational Title | CSIP Role | CTQ/VOC Issue | Influence |
|---|---|---|---|
| CIO | Sponsor | Delivering to business needs | Direct |
| Application Development Director | Internal Supplier | Meeting production dates, effective design and seamless handoff | Direct |
| Operations Director | Champion | Efficient, timely, cost-effective delivery | Direct |
| Business Unit Leadership | Customer | Making the financial plan | Indirect |
| External Supplier | Vendor | Customer satisfaction, profitable engagement | Indirect |

Table C.9 Simplified Project Stakeholder Matrix

## C.21 Project charter

A well defined project charter is essential to gain support and is critical to the success of the initiative. If more groups report to different vice presidents each of whom has their own and often conflicting objectives, a charter is the only means by which all the concerns can be documented.

In the Define phase, a preliminary project charter should clearly outline:
- the product or process affected and benefits expected
- objectives and goals in terms of quality, productivity and business (financial) results expected
- an initial problem statement
- scope and initial budget
- sponsoring individual and organization
- team members and responsibilities
- timelines, milestones, anticipated completion date and required support

This can be further extended over the Analyze phase.

## C.22 Reporting: documenting and training

The people involved or affected by the improved service should be engaged in the documentation and training process. Project reporting helps groom the process owner and sets his/her expectations for managing the newly improved process. Additionally, involving staff in the documentation process instills a sense of ownership among stakeholders. This encourages use of documentation and an on-going commitment to the discipline of documentation. The document should explain:
- background to the project (why it was initiated)
- what has been done to improve the situation, who has been involved
- the results of the project
- the new process
- how to use and read the charts and reports
- who is notified of issues

- when issues are escalated
- the owner of the document and the service

An important aspect of reporting is showing the results, as mentioned in the reporting section of Chapter 2; if the success of the project is shared among peers, this may generate spin-offs or fuel other projects under consideration.

# C.23 Risk Monitoring

The risk levels (that directly influence the trust level) are monitored on an ongoing basis to ensure that the current risk levels are in line with desired risk level.

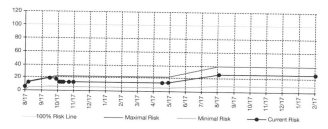

Figure C.12 Risk monitoring

The lines in Figure C.12 mean the following:

- **System's Maximal Risk** is a calculated value that expresses the maximal financial damage that may be caused to the system's assets due to the identified threats. It reflects the potential risks of all threats to the system's assets and is displayed in dollar value as well as in percentage of the total system assets.
- **System's Minimal Risk (Minimal Financial Damage)** is a calculated value that expresses the financial damage that may be caused to

the system's assets and the remaining risks of all threats after full implementation of all mitigation plans. It is displayed in dollar value as well as in percentage of the total system assets.

- **System's Current Risk** is a calculated value that expresses the financial damage that may be caused to the system's assets according to the current implementation level of mitigation plans. It is displayed in dollar value as well as in percentage of the total system assets.

## C.24 SIPOC

If issues identified in Voice of the Customer surveys span multiple departments in both business and technology, any planned intervention first needs to help all groups see the issues at a high, process level perspective. Failure here may cloud the problem and overlook potential improvement opportunities.

A SIPOC model can be developed. A SIPOC is a high-level process map where:

**S** = Suppliers, such as people, materials, information and resources that will be used in the process

**I** = Inputs, the 'raw materials' that are essentially acted upon or changed in the process

**P** = Process, which is the sequence of activities and tasks that actually transform the inputs into a value-add product

**O** = Outputs, being the end product of the process used by the down stream customer, whether internal or external

**C** = Customer, which is the recipient or consumer of the process output

The visual nature of a SIPOC offers several advantages in defining the problem:

- it provides a basis to better understand the problem and thus the potential opportunity
- by using a process discipline, it helps put the functional and organizational barriers in perspective

• it helps to clearly illustrate interdependencies among the different groups

## C.25 Stratification and measurement assessment tree

A Measurement Assessment Tree may be used to evaluate the metrics that will be required to measure each of the requirements. Similar to the CTQ Tree, this tool uses the stratified requirements that were used for the Traceability Matrix and/or the QFD to evaluate the value, usefulness and feasibility of gathering the measure.

The tree starts with the stratified requirements on the left. The data to be measured is listed to the right. As the tree branches, the information is further decomposed into the probable source for each measure. This is critical as the measure is useless if there is no means to record the data.

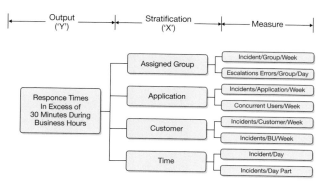

Figure C.13 Sample Measurement Assessment Tree

Evaluating the measures will require careful consideration of the feasibility of collecting the measures. Issues that must be considered are:

- data availability
- number of data points
- accuracy
- complexity
- cost of collecting the data
- repeatability
- reproducibility
- stability of the data

It is helpful if the exercise is started with a visual representation of the tree to facilitate easy discussion and review. When dealing with a large number of measures, however, the graphical tree structure might get in the way of tracking the status of each measure. Here a spreadsheet provides a tracking mechanism.

## C.26 Threat model

Figure C.14 demonstrates a threat model analyzing what influences the trust or security breaches. It describes the interrelations between a threat and the assets, vulnerabilities and countermeasures entities.

The threat causes damage to Asset-1 and Asset-2 and exploits two vulnerabilities: Vulnerability-1 and Vulnerability-2. Vulnerability-1 is mitigated by Countermeasure-1 and Vulnerability-2 is mitigated by Countermeasure-2 and Countermeasure-3 as noted by the arrows pointing towards the vulnerabilities.

Since a threat may exploit several vulnerabilities, the set of possible countermeasures that might mitigate a threat is completely defined by the set of vulnerabilities used in a threat scenario, and is noted by the uninterrupted arrows in the scheme.

| Process | Process Step | Discription | SLR | Goal | Formula | Owner | Responsible | Available? | Automated? | Predictive? | Reporting Metric | Continuous | Event Driven | Sampling | Daily | Weekly | Monthly | Quarterly | Annual | Other | Expection Action |
|---|---|---|---|---|---|---|---|---|---|---|---|---|---|---|---|---|---|---|---|---|---|
| Incident | Detection | Detect Incident | 98%<2 Min | 95% | Percentile | Kevin | Kevin | Y | Y | Y | % | | X | 100% | X | X | X | X | X | | |
| | Response | Respond to Incident | 90%<15 Min | 80% | Percentile | Kevin | Kevin | Y | N | Y | % | | X | 100% | | | X | X | X | | |
| | Functional Escalation | Escalate Incident to Correct Functional Group | 98% Correct | 95% | See Note | Kevin | Kevin | N | N | Y | % | X | X | 100% | | | X | X | X | | |
| | Hierarchical Escalation | Escalate Incident in Breach of SL to Appropriate Management | 98%<5 Min | 95% | See Note | Kevin | Kevin | N | N | Y | % | X | X | 100% | | | X | X | X | | |
| | Notification | Notify Customers | 95%<15 Min | 90% | See Note | Kevin | Kevin | N | N | N | % | | X | 100% | X | X | X | X | X | | |
| | | Notify Management | 98%<5 Min | 95% | See Note | Kevin | Kevin | N | N | N | % | | X | 100% | X | X | X | X | X | | |
| | | Notify Users | 95%<30 Min | 90% | See Note | Kevin | Kevin | N | N | N | % | | X | 100% | X | X | X | X | X | | |

Table C.10 Sample measures audit or tracking and evaluation spreadsheet

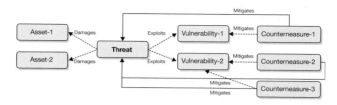

Figure C.14 Threat model

# C.27 Traceability matrix-requirements mapping

The mapping process translates the customer CTQs documented in the initial interview process into specific requirements categories as listed below:

- Business Requirements (BR) describe on the business purpose. In the hierarchy of specifications, these high-level requirements describe what business purpose or objective is to be enabled by the application or service.
- Functional Requirements (FR) define the actions or tasks to be carried out by the application.
- Non-Functional Requirements (NFR) are the system-level requirements such as availability, serviceability and security.
- Technical Requirements (TR) describe what is required of the technology to be used in terms of the interface, standards, performance or capacity of the infrastructure.

Such a rigorous and critical evaluation of the CTQs is essential to fully defining the problem to be addressed by Operations. As with any categorization exercise, requirements stratification ensures a complete understanding of the customer needs.

It may also be valuable to elaborate each of the requirements in terms of any business, functional or technical constraints such as those that may be imposed by compliance, environmental or hardware standards or limitations.

Customer dissatisfaction is often simply a failure to document and track accurately how the designed technology solution actually addresses the business's functional, and non-functional, requirements. It is apparent that such a mapping tool is vitally important to Operations.

Building a traceability matrix requires that each CTQ is documented in a spreadsheet or data base. This document should be managed throughout the life of the project and will serve as the fundamental inputs to the Quality Function Deployment (QFD) Matrix (see section C.14).

Table C.11 illustrates a sample traceability matrix. Notice the CTQs are documented and expanded upon in a descriptions field. Though the expanded description is important as it adds depth and meaning, it should be validated with the customer.

| CTQ | Expanded Description | Categorized Requirements | | | |
|-----|----------------------|----|----|-----|----|
| | | BR | FR | NFR | TR |
| Effective change management | Effective, easy to use - adds value to all stakeholders | | | | |
| | Keep CMDB current | | | | |
| | Changes prioritized to enable resource alignment | | | | |
| | Change system available 7X24 | | | | |
| Reduced Time to Market | Get service running faster | | | | |
| Improved Availability | Honor availability commitments | | | | |
| | Reduce outages | | | | |

Table C.11 Traceability matrix

Each expanded description is then linked to one or more requirements. One expanded description might rank with two or more requirements. The matrix then accompanies all work associated with developing or improving the service to ensure the CTQs are properly recognized and addressed throughout the project.

## C.28   Trust index

A trust index (Figure C.15) gives direct reflection of the ground reality on the effectiveness of security controls.

| Measurement criteria | Weightage | Rating | Weighted rating |
|---|---|---|---|
| % preventive, detective and corrective controls implemented out of the total controls desired. | 0.2 | 3 | 0.6 |
| Number of security incidents | 0.1 | 3 | 0.3 |
| Average time to respond to security incidents | 0.1 | 4 | 0.4 |
| Average time to resolve security incidents | 0.2 | 3 | 0.6 |
| Average security awareness training hours per person | 0.1 | 5 | 0.5 |
| Unplanned downtime due to security incidents | 0.3 | 4 | 1.2 |
| **Trust index** | | | 3.6 |

| Rating | Gap between current and target |
|---|---|
| 1 | More than 50 % |
| 2 | 30 % to 50 % |
| 3 | 10 % to 29 % |
| 4 | 0 % < up to 9 % |
| 5 | 0 % |

Figure C.15 Consolidated trust index

## C.29 Use case

Use cases are commonly adopted by developers and system architects to understand the functional requirements of a system in terms of the goals of a specific interaction with the system. A use case presents requirements in terms of the individual or entity (actor) that interacts with a system. The process architect may evaluate the requirement, the actor and the interaction with the system from an IT Service Management perspective, allowing him to identify those ITSM processes that must be in place to support the requirement. Figure C.16 shows a use case diagram, illustrating the 'actors' and their respective interface requirements to make a change.

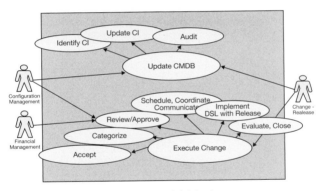

Figure C.16 Use case diagram showing 'actors' and their interfaces

The power of a use case is well known among system architects. Process architects too, should learn to tap the power of this tool and not restrict themselves to the familiar process mapping and design tools. It is the architect of the system who must ensure that the system delivers against the specifications. The architect's expertise lies at the heart of system availability, scalability and specifications compliance. It only makes sense that the process architect should work hand-in-hand with the system architect to ensure that the underlying processes, skills and interfaces are designed to support the architectural design.

You may wish to assign a weighted value to each process to help prioritize the underlying processes as shown in Table C.12. This is a weighted matrix that aligns the required ITSM processes with the specifications or use cases as documented in the traceability matrix.

| Use case traceability matrix specification => | Abbreviation | Keep CMDB current | Prioritize changes | Time-to-market | Reduce outages |
|---|---|---|---|---|---|
| ITSM process | | | | | |
| Configuration | CF | 9 | 3 | 9 | 3 |
| Capacity | CP | 6 | 3 | 9 | 3 |
| Financial | FM | 1 | 6 | 6 | 1 |
| Service Level | SL | 3 | 9 | 6 | 6 |
| Availability | AM | 3 | 9 | 6 | 6 |
| Change | CM | 9 | 9 | 6 | 6 |
| Release | RM | 9 | 9 | 6 | 3 |
| Incident | IM | 1 | 3 | 1 | 6 |
| Problem | PM | 1 | 3 | 1 | 9 |

Table C.12 Weighted matrix to help prioritize ITSM processes

The use case compels a thorough consideration of the infrastructure processes that will be required to meet the customer requirements and a detailed process map will provide insight as to the viability of any processes underlying the use cases.

Use cases are particularly helpful in evaluating the personnel skills. With its focus on actor interaction with the system and the underlying processes that must be in place to meet the system goal or objective, the use case immediately draws attention to both the process and the individual or functional group that interacts with the processes.

The change agent should exercise diligence in defining the basic skills required. ITIL provides a starting point for the high-level roles and responsibilities of, for example, a capacity or problem manager. The use case, however, will impose a more critical thought process at the task level. This detail may be used to define the task level skills and procedural level (Standard Operating Procedures - SOP) documentation that must be defined. The follow-on activities will generally include personnel training and procedural documentation.

## C.30 Voice of the Customer survey

Voice of the Customer (VOC) assists in identifying appropriate Service Improvement Programs (SIP) to gather customer requirements and quantify the Cost of Poor Quality, helping initiate the right SIP supporting CTQ processes.

This is an important survey in both the Define ('what should be improved?') and the Control phase ('does the improvement affect Customer Satisfaction as expected?') to capture ideas, opinions, and feedback. It helps identify CTQ requirements.

Who should be surveyed? Or, in other words, who is the customer? ITIL simply defines customer as the budget-holder, while in process theory, customer may be any downstream recipient or beneficiary of an upstream process or sub-process. Every organization will need to define its own customers in the Define phase. Those customers might actually be people buying an organization's products, but also a sample of each of the user communities in the retail environment. This information then may help feed the SLA process, ensuring that SLAs focus on the experience of those employees who deal directly with the customer and are not skewed by perceptions of head office employees.

Also, participants with intimate knowledge of their respective processes might participate, as well as high-level supervisors to ensure they have visibility to the exercise and have the opportunity to contribute. Supervisor participation is critical since it is this group that will be tapped for resources and budget if the results of the exercise establish the direction for an improvement initiative.

A Voice of the Customer survey can be executed in different ways:
- through website
- through e-mail
- through phone calls
- through conference call
- through face-to-face interviews
- through group meeting or workshop

## C.31 Y=f(X) Equation

This formula was introduced in Chapter 4. We give an example of how to use it here. If you wish to enhance user trust in your ICT applications (part of ICT Security Management), the dependent process outcome Y is trust in the ICT application. Independent Xs to be controlled are:
- Confidentiality (C)
- Integrity(I)
- Availability(A)

So, the formula should now read:

$$User\ trust = f(Confidentiality + Integrity + Availability)$$

For all these 'X-factors', a Critical to Quality (CTQ) can be defined, as listed in Table C.13.

| The Xs | Description | Type of App. | Requirements | |
|---|---|---|---|---|
| | | | Must Have | Nice to Have |
| Confidentiality | Unauthorized access and disclosure may not be possible. | *Business Critical* | Strong 2 factor authentication. Limited login attempts. Need to Know access control. Complete Audit trail. | Biometric Identification. Single Sign On. One time passwords. |
| | | *Non-Critical* | Password Aging. Need to Know access control. | Single Sign On. Audit Trail. |
| Integrity | Unauthorized modifications may not be possible. | *Business Critical* | Control to detect unauthorized modifications. Control for Non-Repudiation. | Controls to prevent unauthorized modifications. |
| | | *Non-Critical* | Controls to detect unauthorized modifications. | |
| Availability | Availability of ICT application services should be sufficient. | *Business Critical* | < 30 minutes downtime per month. < 3 downtime incidents per month. DR & BCP for selected functions. | DR & BCP for all functions. DR & BCP for selected functions. |
| | | *Non-Critical* | < 120 minutes downtime per month. < 8 downtime incidents per month. | |

Table C.13 Need categorization and CTQ identification

For each CTQ, a number of measures are determined, as Table C.14 shows. These performance standards can be used in the Control phase to develop a trust index that reflects the state of security governance of ICT applications.

| Y | The X's | Measures | Performance standard | |
|---|---------|----------|---------|---------|
| | | | Current | Target |
| Trust | Confidentiality - unauthorized access and disclosure | % preventive, detective and corrective controls implemented out of the total controls desired. | 40.00 % | 100.00 % |
| | | Number of unauthorized access or disclosures incidents. | 20 | 0 |
| | Integrity - Unauthorized modifications | % preventive, detective and corrective controls implemented out of the total controls desired. | 30.00 % | 100.00 % |
| | | Number of unauthorized modification incidents. | 30 | 0 |
| | Availability of services | % preventive, detective and corrective controls implemented out of the total controls desired. | 30.00% | 100.00 |
| | | Unplanned downtime due to security incidents. | 120 minutes | 30 minutes |
| | Common measures across CIA | Number of security incidents. | 50 | 25 |
| | | Average time to respond to security incidents. | 120 minutes | 60 minutes |
| | | Average time to resolve security incidents. | 360 minutes | 240 minutes |
| | | Average security awareness training hours per person. | 30 minutes | 120 minutes |

Table C.14 Measures and performance standards for Y

# Appendix D:
# Further reading

## D.1 Books

- Boer, S. den, R. Andharia, M. Harteveld, L. C. Ho, P. L. Musto, & S. Prickel (2006). *Six Sigma for IT Management.* Zaltbommel: Van Haren Publishing.
- Breyfogle III, F. W. (2003, 2nd edition). *Implementing Six Sigma – Smarter Solutions Using Statistical Methods.* New York: John Wiley & Sons, Inc.
- Breyfogle III, F. W., J. M. Cupello, & B. Meadows (2001). *Managing Six Sigma: A Practical Guide to Understanding, Assessing, and Implementing the Strategy That Yields Bottom-Line Success.* New York: John Wiley & Sons, Inc.
- Brue, G. (2005). *Six Sigma For Managers.* New York: McGraw-Hill.
- Brussee, W. (2004). *Statistics for Six Sigma Made Easy.* New York: McGraw-Hill.
- Chen, C., & H. M. Roth (2004). *The Big Book of Six Sigma Training Games: Proven Ways to Teach Basic DMAIC Principles and Quality Improvement Tools.*   New York: McGraw-Hill.
- Chowdhury, S. (2001). *The Power of Six Sigma.* Chicago: Dearborn Trade Publishing.
- *Combining ITIL® and Six Sigma to Improve Technology Service Management at General Electric* (August 2005). M. Fry, & M. Bott, White Paper. Online available at: http://documents.bmc.com/products/documents/67/60/46760/46760.pdf. Consulted November 8, 2006. GE IT Solutions, & BMC Software, Inc.
- Dugmore, J., & S. Lacy (2003). *A Managers' Guide to Service Management.* London: BSI.
- *Foundations of IT Service Management, based on ITIL®* (2005). Jan van Bon (Ed.), on behalf of itSMF-NL. Zaltbommel: Van Haren Publishing.

- George, M. L. (2003). *Lean Six Sigma for Service : How to Use Lean Speed and Six Sigma Quality to Improve Services and Transactions.* New York: McGraw-Hill.
- George, M. L., D. Rowlands, & B. Kastle (2003). *What is Lean Six Sigma.* New York: McGraw-Hill.
- Harry, M., & R. Schroeder (2000). *Six Sigma.* Frankfurt: Campus Fachbuch.
- Juran, J. M., & A. Blanton (1999, 5th edition). *Juran's Quality Handbook.* New York: McGraw-Hill.
- Keller, P. A. (2004). *Six Sigma Demystified : A Self-Teaching Guide (Demystified).* New York: McGraw-Hill.
- Mendel, T. (October 2003). *Beyond ITIL: Despite Hype Full Implementations Are the Exception.* Cambridge, MA, USA: Giga Research (Forrester).
- Pande, P. S., R. P. Neuman, & R. R. Cavanagh (2000). *The Six Sigma Way: How GE, Motorola, and Other Top Companies are Honing Their Performance.* New York: McGraw-Hill.
- Pande, P. S., R. P. Neuman, & R. R. Cavanagh (2001). *The Six Sigma Way Team Fieldbook: An Implementation Guide for Process Improvement Teams.* New York: McGraw-Hill.
- *Planning to Implement Service Management* (2002). Office of Government Commerce (OCG). London: TSO.
- Pyzdek, Th. (2003, 2nd edition). *The Six Sigma Handbook: The Complete Guide for Greenbelts, Blackbelts, and Managers at All Levels, Revised and Expanded Edition.* New York: McGraw-Hill.
- Pyzdek, Th. (2003). *The Six Sigma Project Planner : A Step-by-Step Guide to Leading a Six Sigma Project Through DMAIC.* New York: McGraw-Hill.
- *Service Support* (2000). Office of Government Commerce (OCG). London: TSO.
- *Service Delivery* (2001). Office of Government Commerce (OCG). London: TSO.

- Sheehy, P., D. Navarro, R. Silvers, V. Keyes, D. Dixon, & D. Picard (2002, 1st edition). *The Black Belt Memory Jogger: A Pocket Guide for Six Sigma Success.* Salem, NH: Goal/QPC.
- Shewhart, W. A. (1931). *Economic Control of Quality of Manufactured Product.* New York: D. van Nostrand Company, Inc.
- Shewhart, W. A. (1939). *Statistical Method from the Viewpoint of Quality Control.* New York: Dover.
- Walton, M., & W. E. Deming (1986). *The Deming management method.* New York: Perigee Books.
- Welch, J., & J. A. Byrne (2001). *Jack: Straight from the Gut.* New York: Warner Books, Inc.

## D.2 Websites

- **www.BPtrends.com** - a BPM knowledge database, source for the links to other methodologies.
- **www.isixsigma.com** - a Six Sigma knowledge database website, also see **www.software.isixsigma.com**.
- **www.sixsigmazone.com** - Platform with the latest news about Six Sigma in general.
- **http://en.itsmportal.net** - a knowledge service and a community-of-practice for the subject of management of IT Services.